ALSO BY DR. JENNIFER GILBERT

Books
Churchin' Ain't Easy (2011)
And Deliver Us from People (2012)

Music
Can I Just Be Me? (Musical Single) (2010)
Love Covers All (C.J. Worshippers Music CD) (2012)

DVD
Comedy
Exalted Praise Worship Center Comedy Show (2012)

Preaching
The Value of My Cave Experience—Church
of the Living God (Waco, 2012)

FOR THE PERFECTING OF THE SAINTS

The Five Biblical Ministry Gifts and What They Mean to You

DR. JENNIFER GILBERT

iUniverse LLC
Bloomington

FOR THE PERFECTING OF THE SAINTS
THE FIVE BIBLICAL MINISTRY GIFTS AND WHAT THEY MEAN TO YOU

iUniverse books may be ordered through booksellers or by contacting:

iUniverse LLC
1663 Liberty Drive
Bloomington, IN 47403
www.iuniverse.com
1-800-Authors (1-800-288-4677)

Because of the dynamic nature of the Internet, any web addresses or links contained in this book may have changed since publication and may no longer be valid. The views expressed in this work are solely those of the author and do not necessarily reflect the views of the publisher, and the publisher hereby disclaims any responsibility for them.

Any people depicted in stock imagery provided by Thinkstock are models, and such images are being used for illustrative purposes only. Certain stock imagery © Thinkstock.

ISBN: 978-1-4917-3465-0 (sc)
ISBN: 978-1-4917-3459-9 (e)

Library of Congress Control Number: 2014909487

Printed in the United States of America.

iUniverse rev. date: 05/22/2014

DEDICATION

This book is dedicated to all of the Christian Educators out there, you asked for it and here it is. I pray that this is a blessing to you to read and utilize in your respective forums as a resource as it is for me to write it, let's keep educating to lessen the evil ones manipulating.

CONTENTS

SPECIAL THANKS

To my almighty God for your gifting me in the many areas that he has endowed me. Thank you God for loving me in spite of me. To my children Damaria and J'Donte' Henderson for their undying love and support in my every effort, I could not do it without you. To Ms. Cacean Ballou, thanks for your support as I multi-tasked with our musical project, this book and the million and one other things that I do that involves you and our professional endeavors together. To Prophetess Claudette Gaither for her help and elaboration with this project. I must say that I cannot do my many endeavors alone, in my life it really takes teamwork to make the dream work and my team is my family, my staff and the kingdom laborers that keep me lifted in prayer at all times. Thank you all so much!

EPIGRAPH

Remember people are not as concerned about what
you know unless it lines up with what you show!

-Jennifer

1 Corinthians 12:1

*Now concerning spiritual gifts, brethren,
I would not have you ignorant.*

FOREWORD

I have watched as God began to lay the foundation of order for this end time revival that I believe we are about to see. It is going to be an explosive growth of evangelism this country has not seen before. I believe we are in the beginning stages of the return of our Lord and Savior Jesus Christ. The body of Christ has shifted and become, in my observation, very Hollywood in its presentation of the gospel putting on more of a production, but lacking the power to carry out God's will and the result of that has become an inner society of what is the latest trend rather than being trendsetters. God began to reveal to me his move to strategically bring things back into perspective and help move ourselves away from a church society of entitlement to the Kingdom of God and his righteousness. The Lord said in II Chronicles 7:14, "If my people, which are called by my name, shall humble themselves, and pray, and seek my face, and turn from their wicked ways; then will I hear from heaven, and will forgive their sin, and will heal their land." I have observed, during this transition into a new year, a shift to a heightened consciousness of believers feeling the frustration of living below their means. It is not by coincidence, if you have purchased this book God has a designed a specific purpose in your life. Ephesians 4:1 declares, "I therefore, the prisoner of the Lord, beseech you that ye walk worthy of the vocation wherewith ye are called." According as he hath chosen us in him before the foundation of the world, that we should be holy and without blame before him in love, you were chosen and created for purpose, but may have not understood your gift, nor your call, but this book will bring you into an awareness of yourself and help you to understand the clarion call of Amos 3:7 "Surely the Lord God will do nothing, but he revealed his secret unto his servants the prophets."

Dr. Jennifer Gilbert's work shines a light of the order of God being restored to its original design and not for individuals to gain popularity, but for the church to walk in power. As Ephesians chapter 4 verse 11-12 declares, "And he gave some, apostles; and some, prophets; and some, evangelists; and some, pastors and teachers; 12 for the perfecting of the saints, for the work of the ministry, for the edifying of the body of Christ." This book will begin to line you up with the purpose God has for your life. I have seen and heard many writers who try to joggle unsuccessfully the balance of spiritual revelation and life application, but Dr. Jennifer Gilbert hits a home run with this book. I find it rewarding when one dares to stand boldly and declare God's word in this hour. Dr. Gilbert is going to challenge you in your walk, and have you to understand the attributes to one's office and associate it with the gifts and help you activate them that you may began to develop and to serve your purpose with vitality. I believe the Lord has sanctioned Dr. Jennifer Gilbert to carry the mantle to bring the body of Christ into the unlocking of the impossible and to empower the church for the 21st century and beyond.

Bishop Gregory Thomas
City of Bryan Church of the Living God
Bryan, Texas

PREFACE

This work is another favorite of mine. My first book, *Churchin' Ain't Easy* was one for the new converts or maybe even old ones who needed to be realigned with the will of God. My second book, *And Deliver Us From People*, was a crossover book that everyone could use in their homes, workplaces, churches and anywhere else that they encounter people. This book speaks to my kind, the ones who are saved and seeking for a deeper meaning to life and a greater understanding of their calling. I have heard many people speak of the five-fold ministry and there are many people out there that don't even know what it is, let alone those out there who refute it even though it is a biblical concept.

Ephesians 4:11-16

11And he gave some, apostles; and some, prophets; and some, evangelists; and some, pastors and teachers;

12For the perfecting of the saints, for the work of the ministry, for the edifying of the body of Christ:

13Till we all come in the unity of the faith, and of the knowledge of the Son of God, unto a perfect man, unto the measure of the stature of the fullness of Christ:

14That we henceforth be no more children, tossed to and fro, and carried about with every wind of doctrine, by the sleight of men, and cunning craftiness, whereby they lie in wait to deceive;

15But speaking the truth in love, may grow up into him in all things, which is the head, even Christ:

16From whom the whole body fitly joined together and compacted by that which every joint supplieth, according to the effectual working in the measure of every part, maketh increase of the body unto the edifying of itself in love.

This book will explain personal, spiritual and even some professional characteristics of individuals who possess these gifts and/or callings and the ways in which they operate. I was so honored that God chose to use me for this work, something that has not been done before but also something that is vitally needed in the body of Christ. The bible states;

<u>Proverbs 4:7</u>

Wisdom is the principal thing; therefore get wisdom: and with all thy getting get understanding.

With this book, I pray that you will gain knowledge of the material, wisdom for the application and understanding of yourself. Perhaps you have always done a thing and didn't know why, this book may help you to understand that indeed you were called from your mother's womb which means that you may have exhibited some of these behaviors, even as a child.

<u>Jeremiah 1:5</u>

Before I formed thee in the belly I knew thee; and before thou camest forth out of the womb I sanctified thee, and I ordained thee a prophet unto the nations.

INTRODUCTION

What makes this book necessary is the lack of instruction in reference to this subject manner. Few people really talk about the five-fold ministry, let alone teach about it. This book seeks to educate all members of the body, even leadership on the matters of the ministry gifts and the vital role that they play in the success of the church.

I have worked in the gifting as well as the callings of the five-fold ministry gifts for over 30 years and it has been a challenge because it is a truth that many don't teach on so therefore, many don't understand it. The five-fold ministry gifts are those of the;

Teacher
Pastor
Evangelist
Prophet/ess
Apostle

The number 5 is critical! There were . . .

- 5 books of the Pentateuch
- 5 attributes of God (Wonderful, Counselor, Almighty God, Everlasting Father, Prince of Peace
- 5 points on a star
- The number of grace

- 5 witnesses to the birth of Christ (Mary, Joseph, the 3 wise men
- There were five wounds incurred on Calvary (right and left hand and foot, the piercing in his side)
- All elements of the earth was done by the 5th day to release power and authority
- Now we are looking at the five-fold ministry

The five-fold ministry gifts are alive, well, functioning and advancing. A perspective gained through continued experience in and with the concept as well as through personal observation. All of the positions are allowing the church an upright and balanced stance in both the defensive and offensive arenas. A stance that is allowing us to be advantageously victorious as we pursue and subdue enemy forces, namely, Lucifer and his satanic hoard and that including the "***Counterfeit Five-fold***," yes, there is a counterfeit. A demonic structure specifically designed to do exactly what John 10:10 speaks of "steal, kill and destroy."

John 10:10

10The thief cometh not, but for to steal, and to kill, and to destroy: I am come that they might have life, and that they might have it more abundantly.

Before we begin this literary venture I want to establish a few definitions within the title alone.

Vitality-the capacity for survival or the continuation of a meaningful or purposeful existence. Power to live and grow.

Ministry-something that serves as an agency, instrument, or means

Gift-something bestowed or acquired without any particular effort by the recipient or without it being earned

I believe that it is important for us to know these facts in order for us to fully grasp the connection that God wants us to embark upon in this book. My passion is education in general but specifically Christian Education and I believe all of the word but especially when it says that people perish for the lack of knowledge. I have been in ministry for a number of years and have seen the tragic effects of ignorance when it comes to the word of God and the execution, implementation and instruction therein. In fact my dissertation is on this very matter. The effects that a relevant Christian education program has on church membership attainment and retention. Basically my theory is that if you adequately teach them, they will come and be faithful in their coming but you have to be real, relevant and reputable in your approach.

Hosea 4:6

My people are destroyed for lack of knowledge: because thou hast rejected knowledge, I will also reject thee, that thou shalt be no priest to me: seeing thou hast forgotten the law of thy God, I will also forget thy children.

III John 1:2

2Beloved, I wish above all things that thou mayest prosper and be in health, even as thy soul prospereth.

In my previous books I intentionally didn't put a lot of scripture for the sake of making the reading a bit easier but this particular work will be inundated with scripture to ensure that once you identify your gift that you can actually look for biblical passages and individuals that deal with or walk in that calling for the sake of identification and clarification.

People of God, it is vital that we find, know, understand and learn not only our individual positions within the body of Christ, but how the body as a whole is structured and functions including the five-fold ministry gifts. Lack of such knowledge and understanding leaves us vulnerable, open prey for satanic attack and manipulation of our God given gifts, thus causing individual and church hindrance. Believe it or not there are people out there who don't recognize nor acknowledge the gifting that Christ has put in place to assist us in kingdom advancement. There is no need to argue, nor belabor about the issue. Jesus, himself, encountered this mindset (blatant refusal to receive or believe) in his hometown (resistance and such that the Bible records in Matthew 13:58).

Matthew 13:58

*58And he did not many mighty works
there because of their unbelief.*

Jesus knowing that we too, those who would follow after him, would experience like situations (Matthew 10:24, 25).

Matthew 10:24, 25

24The disciple is not above his master, nor the servant above his lord.

25It is enough for the disciple that he be as his master, and the servant as his lord. If they have called the master of the house Beelzebub, how much more shall they call them of his household?

Upon his ascension he secured and released back to us (his church) tools called ministry gifts that would enable us to accomplish and fulfill Ephesians 4:8-18.

Ephesians 4:8-18

8Wherefore he saith, When he ascended up on high, he led captivity captive, and gave gifts unto men.

9(Now that he ascended what it is but that he also descended first into the lower parts of the earth?

10He that descended is the same also that ascended up far above all heavens, that he might fill all things.)

11And he gave some, apostles; and some, prophets; and some, evangelists; and some, pastors and teachers;

12For the perfecting of the saints, for the work of the ministry, for the edifying of the body of Christ:

13Till we all come in the unity of the faith, and of the knowledge of the Son of God, unto a perfect man, unto the measure of the stature of the fullness of Christ:

14That we henceforth be no more children, tossed to and fro, and carried about with every wind of doctrine, by the sleight of men, and cunning craftiness, whereby they lie in wait to deceive;

15But speaking the truth in love, may grow up into him in all things, which is the head, even Christ:

16From whom the whole body fitly joined together and compacted by that which every joint supplieth, according to the effectual working in the measure of every part, maketh increase of the body unto the edifying of itself in love.

17This I say therefore, and testify in the Lord, that ye henceforth walk not as other Gentiles walk, in the vanity of their mind,

18Having the understanding darkened, being alienated from the life of God through the ignorance that is in them, because of the blindness of their heart:

<u>NOTE</u>

Within the structure of this book, you will see a section that speaks of new converts. This term has a vast definition. It can range from babes (someone who is completely an infant when it comes to Jesus, Salvation, the church etc.) then there are those that are quite fluent to Christ and the things of God but they just need to be transformed into the kingdom work. A great example would be Saul before he became Paul in Acts Chapter 9 especially in versus 20). Distinction should be made in reference to the level of exposure one can handle to the various gifts especially that of the prophet.

<u>Acts 9</u>

1And Saul, yet breathing out threatenings and slaughter against the disciples of the Lord, went unto the high priest,

2And desired of him letters to Damascus to the synagogues, that if he found any of this way, whether they were men or women, he might bring them bound unto Jerusalem.

3And as he journeyed, he came near Damascus: and suddenly there shined round about him a light from heaven:

4And he fell to the earth, and heard a voice saying unto him, Saul, Saul, why persecutest thou me?

5And he said, Who art thou, Lord? And the Lord said, I am Jesus whom thou persecutest: it is hard for thee to kick against the pricks.

6And he trembling and astonished said, Lord, what wilt thou have me to do? And the Lord said unto him, Arise, and go into the city, and it shall be told thee what thou must do.

7And the men which journeyed with him stood speechless, hearing a voice, but seeing no man.

8And Saul arose from the earth; and when his eyes were opened, he saw no man: but they led him by the hand, and brought him into Damascus.

9And he was three days without sight, and neither did eat nor drink.

10And there was a certain disciple at Damascus, named Ananias; and to him said the Lord in a vision, Ananias. And he said, Behold, I am here, Lord.

11And the Lord said unto him, Arise, and go into the street which is called Straight, and enquire in the house of Judas for one called Saul, of Tarsus: for, behold, he prayeth,

12And hath seen in a vision a man named Ananias coming in, and putting his hand on him, that he might receive his sight.

13Then Ananias answered, Lord, I have heard by many of this man, how much evil he hath done to thy saints at Jerusalem:

14And here he hath authority from the chief priests to bind all that call on thy name.

15But the Lord said unto him, Go thy way: for he is a chosen vessel unto me, to bear my name before the Gentiles, and kings, and the children of Israel:

16For I will shew him how great things he must suffer for my name's sake.

17And Ananias went his way, and entered into the house; and putting his hands on him said, Brother Saul, the Lord, even Jesus, that appeared unto thee in the way as thou camest, hath sent me, that thou mightest receive thy sight, and be filled with the Holy Ghost.

18And immediately there fell from his eyes as it had been scales: and he received sight forthwith, and arose, and was baptized.

19And when he had received meat, he was strengthened. Then was Saul certain days with the disciples which were at Damascus.

20And straightway he preached Christ in the synagogues, that he is the Son of God.

21But all that heard him were amazed, and said; Is not this he that destroyed them which called on this name in Jerusalem, and came hither for that intent, that he might bring them bound unto the chief priests?

22But Saul increased the more in strength, and confounded the Jews which dwelt at Damascus, proving that this is very Christ.

23And after that many days were fulfilled, the Jews took counsel to kill him:

24But their laying await was known of Saul. And they watched the gates day and night to kill him.

25Then the disciples took him by night, and let him down by the wall in a basket.

26And when Saul was come to Jerusalem, he assayed to join himself to the disciples: but they were all afraid of him, and believed not that he was a disciple.

27But Barnabas took him, and brought him to the apostles, and declared unto them how he had seen the Lord in the way, and that he had spoken to him, and how he had preached boldly at Damascus in the name of Jesus.

28And he was with them coming in and going out at Jerusalem.

29And he spake boldly in the name of the Lord Jesus, and disputed against the Grecians: but they went about to slay him.

30Which when the brethren knew, they brought him down to Cæsarea, and sent him forth to Tarsus.

31Then had the churches rest throughout all Judæa and Galilee and Samaria, and were edified; and walking in the fear of the Lord, and in the comfort of the Holy Ghost, were multiplied.

32And it came to pass, as Peter passed throughout all quarters, he came down also to the saints which dwelt at Lydda.

33And there he found a certain man named Æneas, which had kept his bed eight years, and was sick of the palsy.

34And Peter said unto him, Æneas, Jesus Christ maketh thee whole: arise, and make thy bed. And he arose immediately.

35And all that dwelt at Lydda and Saron saw him, and turned to the Lord.

36Now there was at Joppa a certain disciple named Tabitha, which by interpretation is called Dorcas: this woman was full of good works and almsdeeds which she did.

37And it came to pass in those days, that she was sick, and died: whom when they had washed, they laid her in an upper chamber.

38And forasmuch as Lydda was nigh to Joppa, and the disciples had heard that Peter was there, they sent unto him two men, desiring him that he would not delay to come to them.

39Then Peter arose and went with them. When he was come, they brought him into the upper chamber: and all the widows stood by him weeping, and shewing the coats and garments which Dorcas made, while she was with them.

40But Peter put them all forth, and kneeled down, and prayed; and turning him to the body said, Tabitha, arise. And she opened her eyes: and when she saw Peter, she sat up.

41And he gave her his hand, and lifted her up, and when he had called the saints and widows, presented her alive.

42And it was known throughout all Joppa; and many believed in the Lord.

43And it came to pass, that he tarried many days in Joppa with one Simon a tanner.

BOOK STRUCTURE

Integrated within the structure of this book is research that I have performed on the importance of education in the Christian arena. Many times we see church as an opportunity to feel good but lack the understanding of the vitality of the education that is needed to live a successful Christian life. You will see some academic references as well as biblical reference to this literary experience. The tone may be a little different but the power therein will be a greater magnitude as we embark upon a well rounded learning experience. This research can be used to help to grow your church as well as implement an educational environment within the church location and structure. In the times that we are living in, we need more than just Sunday school and Bible study but the need to grasp a concrete understanding of the operation of Kingdom principles and methodologies are crucial.

The Vitality of
Christian Education

Education in its simplest form

Learning involves acquiring and modifying knowledge, skills, strategies, beliefs, attitudes, behaviors and theory with a scientifically acceptable set of principles offered to explain a phenomenon. For the sake of this literary experience the acquiring of biblically sound knowledge will induce a modification of former knowledge (give a new way of seeing things), and create new skills (coping mechanisms to handle life's issues). It will also introduce new strategies of how to educate others as well as conduct personal devotions and rituals for spiritual growth.

Learning is an enduring change in behavior, or in the capacity to behave in a given fashion, which results from practice or other forms of experience (Schunk, 2008). Optimally, when one does better they often compel others to follow that same pattern of behavior of finding a better way of doing a thing. One criterion for defining learning is a behavioral change or change in the capacity for behavior (Schunk, 2008). People learn when they become capable of doing and/or thinking something differently. Learning involves developing new actions or modifying existing ones (Schunk, 2008). For some this could mean adopting new beliefs or replacing old ones with a more biblically sound or correct implementation.

A second criterion inherent in this definition is that behavioral change (or capacity for change) endures over time (Schunk, 2008). This attests to the need for a consistent structural education program to assist in the continuum of the new practice which will in time become a habit and ultimately a lifestyle. The more a person is instructed on a matter the more precise they become and the less of a task the new behavior generates. A third criterion is that learning occurs through practice or other forms of experience (e.g., observing others and engaging in learning activities) (Schunk, 2008).

Learning is a permanent change in behavior or as knowledge acquired by study (Galbraith & Fouch, 2007). Learning can be formal or informal and is usually motivated by an individual's transitions and experiences.

The Bible Belt

The Bible belt is the southern portions of the United States which is also the region that is most likely to fall prey to the manipulation tactics of the enemy. The reason, in my opinion that they are more suseptble to fall prey is because they are the most religious but the least educated in the Christian arena. Think of all of the incidents that have happened in this region;
David Koresh – He was the American leader of the Branch Davidians religious sect, believing himself to be its final prophet. Howell legally changed his name to David Koresh on May 15, 1990 Koresh being the Persian name of Cyrus the Great. A 1993 raid by the U.S. Bureau of Alcohol, Tobacco, Firearms and Explosives, and the subsequent siege by the FBI ended with the burning of the Branch Davidian ranch outside of Waco, Texas,

in McLennan County. Koresh, 54 other adults, and 28 children were found dead after the fire.

Jim Jones-*(though this took place in Africa many of the people originated from the Bible belt region of the U.S.)* Jones ordered everyone to assemble at the pavilion. Once everyone was assembled, Jones spoke to his congregation. He was in a panic and seemed agitated. He was upset that some of his members had left. He acted like things had to happen in a hurry. He told the congregation that there was to be an attack on Ryan's group. He also told them that because of the attack, Jonestown wasn't safe. Jones was sure that the U.S. government would react strongly to the attack on Ryan's group. "[W]hen they start parachuting out of the air, they'll shoot some of our innocent babies," Jones told them. Jones told his congregation that the only way out was to commit the "revolutionary act" of suicide. One woman spoke up against the idea, but after Jones offered reasons why there was no hope in other options, the crowd spoke out against her. When it was announced that Ryan was dead, Jones became more urgent and more heated. Jones urged the congregation to commit suicide by saying, "If these people land out here, they'll torture some of our children here. They'll torture our people, they'll torture our seniors. We cannot have this." Jones told everyone to hurry. Large kettles filled with grape flavored Flavor-Aid (not Kool-Aid), cyanide, and Valium were placed in the open-sided pavilion. Babies and children were brought up first. Syringes were used to pour the poisoned juice into their mouths. Mothers then drank some of the poisoned punch. Next went other members. Some members were already dead before others got their drinks. If anyone wasn't cooperative, there were guards with guns and crossbows to encourage them. It took approximately five minutes for each person to die. On that day, November 18, 1978, 912 people died from drinking the poison, 276 of whom were children. Jones died from a single gunshot wound to the head, but it is unclear whether or not he did this himself. Only a handful or so people survived, either by escaping into the jungle or hiding somewhere in the compound.

In total 918 people died, either at the airport or at the Jonestown compound.

Bible Belt Development

Some say that the name "Bible Belt" is due in part to the destitution of the slaves believing that God would bring them out of captivity like he did the children of Israel in Exodus 1. This also leads to the understanding of why the Southern states are generally the most religious states in the U.S. Others say that it is due to the deprivation and economic destitution of that region. The actual reason is unknown but some findings do support a correlation of religion and the faultiness of socioeconomic class across the region (Florida, 2012).

Dimensions of Influence

The three dimensions of influence in the Bible Belt are income, education, and occupation. Florida (2012) states religiosity is higher in lower income states where poverty is a commonplace. Florida (2012) goes on to share that states that the share of states with residents who say religion is very important is correlated with the poverty rate (.60) and negatively associated with the state income levels (-.56).

Florida (2012) also states that religion displays a lower rate of acceptance in the more educated states and is negatively associated with the share of state residents that are college grads (-.55). Crabtree (2013) tells of how intelligence and religiosity correlate and how the more educated a person is, the less religious they tend to be. He also tells of the fact that children of more deeply religious parents have an IQ of 8-10 points less than their counterparts. Florida (2012) goes on to share that religion is also associated with all types of working class jobs (r=.61) and negatively associated with the share of workers doing knowledge, profession and creative work. The United States remains a largely Christian nation with nine out of ten Americans who identify with the Christian religion (Newport, 2012).

Religiosity in the Bible Belt

Christian Education Defined

The word education comes from the Latin word "educare" which means "to educate or train." In its simplest form initially it meant "to lead out." Today, it also implies "to put into someone." According to Lee (2001) Christian education can be defined as the humanitarian discipline that extracts and develops the individual gifts given to one by God which develops special graces, general virtues and general terms of knowledge to be relayed to every person as revealed if Jesus Christ as the incarnate Word of God and supported by scripture. It is the present tradition for churches to have the normal weekly Bible Study and Sunday School. The point and purpose of the book is to advocate for the presence of a more in depth, ongoing, and relevant Christian Education curriculum to increase membership attainment and retention as well as to acquire church and scriptural relativity and relevance.

The purpose of Christian Education

Christian education demands instruction in the many facets of religiosity and spirituality and all that is attained therein. It speaks on religion (teaching about the creator and redeemer). It teachers about philosophy which teaches about creation as a whole. It also speaks to mathematics which teaches of how to count God's creatures and the interaction therein. It teaches the natural sciences like physics and biology to teach how to understand the properties of the things God made. Lastly it teaches history and geography as well as language also including reading and writing each of which teaches about the aspects of creation (Lee, 2001).

In writing this book, the idea of articulating the purpose of a Christian education curriculum could be done by creating and implementing

- Goal-driven instruction
- Effective teaching
- Avoiding the indoctrination of students
- Qualified facilitators

So the lesser and more immediate goal of Christian education must be to acquire knowledge, a specialized knowledge of both Heaven and earth as well as the God who created and redeemed as well as sustains them all (Lee, 2001).

The Benefactors of Christian Education

Leadership

There are many benefactors to the efforts of Christian Education. Starting with the leadership who benefits from the presence of accountability. Leaders are the one who are held accountable for getting to their congregants and the needs that they possess. This serves as the runway for which the entire process begins. Not only does it require accountability for the association of the leader and the congregant but it also forces the leader to educate themselves in order for the transmission of knowledge to take place.

Healthy churches. Churches that are healthy and grow spiritually tend to be socially vibrant and have some significant aspects that create harmony and contentment and the atmosphere is conducive for the church goer to come to church services and fellowship.

The environment will also provoke them to invite others. When a church invokes a feeling of home, members learn and grow. Visitors have a tendency to not only become members but become active members thus leading to a positive Christian experience. Healthy churches prevent negative themes that are significant because they motivate, inspire and cheer people to feel a part of something greater than themselves (Krejcir, 2007).

Research supports that there are seven significant factors to a healthy and vibrant church.

- They are centered upon Christ;
- The members experience the love and fruit that is real, biblical and teach uncompromised truths, which are not polluted with their opinions;
- People have a tendency to feel safe, connected, content, and compelled to learn and grow;
- The teaching ability of the Pastor or leaders propels growth of spiritual knowledge;
- They are built around care and solid biblical, yet relevant preaching and teaching;
- They teach such aspects as holiness, the power of the blood of Jesus, how to handle sin and temptation therein, they also teach how to relate to one another, how to live the biblical precepts of knowledge and living of which are being modeled by the leader;
- The preaching is preached with power, conviction, clarity, passion and truth (Krejcir, 2007).

Healthy churches are proactive in their approach to ministry. They are on the lookout for people who enter in with agendas and attitudes that are contrary to the environment that they are trying to establish. Destructive members are counseled and if they don't stop their activities, then then they are removed from fellowship until they repent.

The fatality of failure. Krejcir (2007) completed several studies but there is one entitled, "Why Churches Succeed" that explain the factors that have been found to associate with healthy churches that have proven successful and healthy and show signs of consistent growth.

Factors that are relevant and important to the transcending of a failing edifice to a successful one are that;

- People come and are stimulated to serve when the Bible is taught in a real, effectual and applicable way;
- People are encouraged to read through the bible, do devotions and practice the disciplines of the faith as modeled by leadership;
- Leadership models passion for their spirituality;
- Leaders continue to model, challenge, and encourage people to grow beyond their own expectations for themselves and from this pool, new leadership is formed and recruited;
- It also speaks as to how effective the outreach and mission is that compels people to serve;
- Churches that are growing have prayer as a primary focus.

U.S. Congregations (2010) tells of the correlation between worship and spirituality. The study correlates the fact that those who attend worship are also doing things in their personal lives to deepen their faith and promote their spiritual growth. Some people attribute their growth in faith to the congregation-worship, bible study, and caring people. Of those that have grown, 43% say they have grown in the past year and the congregation was their reasoning. Only a few of them said that it was due to personal devotions but 4 out of 6 have not experiences significant growth in the last year.

Facilitators

To achieve the status of a true leader one must be able to integrate scholarship and practice. Integrating scholarship and practice means that leaders must maintain theoretical understandings of core leadership principles through scholarly research and study. It also means that they have to be able to convert their theoretical understanding into daily, observable leadership behaviors and practices.

A spiritual leader characterizes genuineness and encourages those in the organization to take risks, so others may see an openness and trust. The spiritual leader views the organization not from a top down perspective, but rather a horizontal view, seeing others as valuable colleagues serving the community with purpose

Students

Student of a Christian education program vary. They range in age, education and ability as well as experience. With the being said, there has to a structure that is accommodating to all parties involved. One such structure could be structured as

- PK-teaching the mere actions of Christ through stories and adventure type modalities
- K-12-teaching the character of Christians and effects of the actions of Christ on their lives
- Teens-teaching the relevancy of religion in relation to decision making and peer pressure and the identification with the attributes of Christianity.
- Adult-teaching the transcendence of prior structures to the point of application of the scripture to their daily lives as well as identification with the attributes of Christianity and the life that they live.

- Leaders-teaching the leadership responsibilities of Christianity and the attributes that they should strive to live by as a living epistle to mankind that provokes emulation and imitation.

This segmentation can be manipulated into any structure but can serve as an example of how to implement a Christian education curriculum that is age and developmentally appropriate for the students.

A Christian Education program does not only have to teach biblical principle but precepts as well. Ensuring that relevancy takes precedence and relativity is at the forefront, educating the various aspects of life such as financial planning, gender identification, marital success and the like.

Program expectations. There is plethora of information of what should be expected in a Christian education classroom and the expectations that each learner should have for the process of partaking in the experience. Forte (2009) speaks to the need of applying theory and human development in the efforts of education in the field of social work but can also be applied to the Christian education curriculum. Understanding and applying theory and human development would assist facilitators in that various manners and approaches that can and should be used to conduct instruction.

There are an unlimited number of frameworks for human development that educators can use to structure how they enrich their courses. Teaching by metaphors, which involves the imaginative and educational use of comparisons between theoretical ideas and everyday events, objects, processes, people and places are one of the most prevalent (Forte, 2009). This is one of the main ways that Christ, himself taught, through parables that resonated with the individuals He was talking to. For instance when he talked to the fisherman that later became disciples and later Apostles, he spoke in aquatic language (Mark 1:17). When he talked to farmers, he spoke in their language (Matthew 13:18-30).

Russell (2006) speaks us on various aspects of adult learning. There are variables that should be integrated into a structured education forum for adults such as

- the characteristics of adult learners
- the reasons why they learn
- Factors which serve as sources of motivation.

Attention has to be brought to the fact that adults have a greater depth, breadth and quality of previous life experience than do younger people. There are also levels of engagement that should take place when an adult learning experience is underway and how to successfully facilitate learning in any modality utilizing the learning styles of the students.

Engaging Christian Education

The teaching and learning experience cannot result in anything meaningful if the learner is not engaged in the process. The greater the engagement, the more significant the potential change in the learner, and the deeper the personal meaning will become for them (Coley, 2012). Bain (2004) states that the best educators thought of teaching as anything they might do to help and encourage students to learn. Teaching is engaging students, and engineering the environment in which they learn.

No great teacher relied solely on lecture, but there are lectures that helped students learn deeply and extensively because they raised questions and won students attention to those issues. The students became engaged in thinking through the problems, in confronting them, in looking at evidence and in reasoning rather than memorizing (Bain, 2004).

Biblical examples. There are several biblical examples that could be used to support the cause of mentorship and education, however, one of the greatest examples would be that of Paul and Timothy.

Paul and Timothy. One of the greatest relationships for mentorship is between Paul and Timothy. Some of the attributes that could be adopted was;

- Paul took Timothy under his tutelage and made it personal
  o *"To Timothy, my beloved child: Grace, mercy, and peace from God the Father and Christ Jesus our Lord. I thank God whom I serve with a clear conscience, as did my fathers, when I remember you constantly in my prayers. As I remember your tears, I long night and day to see you that I may be filled with joy (II Timothy 1:2-4).*
- He knew him personally as well as his lineage and life story
  o *I am reminded of your sincere faith, a faith that dwelt first in your grandmother Lois and your mother Eunice and now, I am sure, dwells in you (II Timothy 1:5).*
- He reminded him of his God given gifts
  o *Hence I remind you to rekindle the gift of God that is within you through the laying on of my hands; for God did not give us a spirit of timidity but a spirit of power and love and self-control" (II Timothy 1:6,7)*
- Paul never feared to review what Timothy had learned through instruction and observation
  o *"Now you have observed my teaching, my conduct, my aim in life, my faith, my patience, my love, my steadfastness, my persecutions, my sufferings, what befell me at Antioch, at Iconium, and at Lystra, what persecutions I endured; yet from them all the Lord rescued me (II Timothy 3:10-11).*
- He warned him of the opposition to come

Indeed all who desire to live a godly life in Christ Jesus will be persecuted, while evil men and impostors will go on from bad to worse, deceivers and deceived. And he continually encouraged him But as for you, continue in what you have learned and have firmly believed, knowing from whom you learned it and how from childhood you have been acquainted with the sacred writings which are able to instruct you for salvation through faith in Christ Jesus" (II Timothy 3:12-15).

Maslows Heirarchy of Needs

Maslow's hierarchy of needs grows from the most basic needs of humans to the peak of the hierarchy which is self-actualization (Brown & Cullen, 2006). This hierarchy not only applies for secular survival of the human well-being, it can also account for the universality of religious practice across culture and time as well as provide additional understanding for the depth of feeling which religion occupies in those who practice it (Brown & Cullen, 2006).

When looking at the pyramid of the hierarchy of needs each level can be a representation of the questions and/or fears of the congregation;

- Physiological needs-Can you provide me with the most basic of instruction to assist in my daily living? We as believers have to understand that if a person is hungry, they can't hear our message of Christ until we meet their immediate basic need of hunger.
- Safety needs-Can I trust you not to lead me astray with your own opinion? This is the point and place where people are looking at your life to see if you live by what you teach and preach about. This is where integrity comes in.
- Belonging and love-Will I have a place to belong where I can share my experiences without judgment, discrimination or ridicule? This is huge in these current times. Many members share things about their struggles and clergy abuses this and often uses it or alludes to it in their next sermon which

13

makes one feel that it is a violation of trust and confidence. There is nothing more devastating then hearing mention or reference to what you said in confidence over the pulpit.

- Esteem-Can you tell me who I am in Christ with Biblical reference and instruction for effective implementation in my life? Many believers seek validation in their life and in all of their longing; their greatest longing is their need to feel important and needed in the body of Christ. This is where rapport and relationship comes in. It is vitally important that their gifts and callings are sought out, educated and used to the glory of God. Believe it or not if we can make them feel needed and validated in the church, then it will trickle over into their personal and professional lives as well.

- Self-actualization-Will you help me become my best, most authentic self? This is the loudest cry of believers and really the human race as a whole. Everyone wants to know that they are on track to being all that God has called and ordained for them to be. Everyone wants to know their purpose and to fulfill it to the best of their ability.

Christian Education Implementations

Russell (2006) explained some key points to remember when embarking upon the implementation of instruction. Some of those points were: convey a desire to connect with the learner, provide a challenge without causing frustration and above all provide feedback and positive reinforcement about what has been learned.

When adult learners have control over the nature, timing, and direction of the learning process, the entire experience is facilitated and more meaningful. They have a need to be self-directed by having a say in what they learn and will often take a leadership role in their learning (Russell, 2006). One way of allowing self-direction is the inclusion of a return demonstration by the learner.

This means giving them an opportunity to show what they know which will correlate to the motivation that they have to learning. Allowing such activities as projects and presentation wherein the learner appears to be the expert has great implications (Russell, 2006).

Barriers to Learning

There will be barriers to every learning experience. The learners have lives outside of the educational setting that can play a major part in the program. Some of these barriers include: lack of time, lack of confidence, lack of information about the opportunities to learn, scheduling problems and lack of motivation (Russell, 2006).

The more relevant educators remain the more they will be in demand. When looking at the framework of this research and the optimal goal, certain correlations can be made. There is a certain relationship between need and achievement that takes place in the lives of learners. Russell (2006) states that most adult learners enter learning experience to create change in their skills, behavior, knowledge level and even their attitudes. Each learner brings to the Christian education learning experience preconceived thoughts and feelings that will affect their learning experience.

How Laypeople Learn

Looking at the general consensus of the average Christian experience, one would be remiss to think that all parishioners learn on the same level, at the same time, using the same modality which would be sermonic presentations given on most Sunday mornings. The truth of the matter is that parishioners learn in different manners. This understanding establishes not only the need of differentiated instruction but also the basis of a more structured and intimate learning environment.

Active Learning

Active learning is a wide range of teaching strategies that engage the learner in the actual instruction that takes place. An active learning classroom is a learning community where all participate, including the teacher (Olrich, 2010).

Olrich (2010) states that typically this methodology yields some of the following;

- Active responses;
- Construction of understanding;
- Higher order thinking;
- Assessments;
- Use of prior experience;
- Physiological change;
- Competition;

A great deal of research since the 1990s has identified metacognition as key to deep thinking and flexible use of knowledge and skills (Schoenbach, 1999). Baumann (2003) states a Biblical Christian educator would be more comfortable saying the learner discovers meaning or builds understanding of truths that already exist. Marti MacCollugh (2003) refers to this interactive learning as the process whereby the learner takes in new information from thier surroundings to begin the process, make sense of it, and stores the information for retrieval and use. Schuttloffel identifies the following three levels of reflection that are interrelated in the metacognitive process:

- The critical level that asked the why questions;
- The interpretive level that response to the what questions;
- The technical level that answers the how questions;

With all of these components in mind one feels more empowered to plan lesson plans for implementation with a structured

Christian Education program, keeping in mind the exercise of learner engagement and participation by all including the teacher.

Cox, Barnum, & Hameloth (2010) outlined a nine point lesson plan format for Christian Education. This formatting is relevantly designed for both professionally and biblically sound and integrative instruction. The nine components that they speak of are the essentials of learning outcomes and are

- A purpose;
- Learner attributes;
- Principles;
- Plan;
- Plan efficacy;
- Practice;
- Citizenship equipping;
- Assessment;

Table 2.1. A Nine Point Lesson Plan Format for Christian Education
(Cox, Barnum, Hameloth, 2010)

Element	Objective
Learning Outcomes	Teachers and students need to know the destination of their educational journey before setting out on it
Purpose	Helps keep education focused and also keeps the student focused.
Learner attributes	The prior knowledge, experience, and attributes that shape the learner's receptivity to the instruction
Principles	Cause and effect relationship, regularity, and generalizability statements
Plan	How the lesson should be taught or presented
Plan efficacy	The power of the lesson
Practice	The actual activities engaged in by the students to help ensure the lessons are permanent
Equipping for citizenship	Helps ensure that the teacher focuses on the contributions of education of education to the nation's, not just the learns' benefit
Assessment	How the student will be evaluated regarding both progress toward and attainment of learning outcomes.

Engaging Christian Education

Engaging the learner in the process can make the learning experience more meaningful. The greater the engagement, the more significant the potential change in the learner, and the deeper the personal meaning will become for them (Coley, 2012). Bain (2004) stated that the best educators thought of teaching as anything they might do to help and encourage students to learn. Teaching is engaging students, and engineering the environment in which they learn.

No great teacher relied solely on lecture, but there are lectures that helped students learn deeply and extensively because they raised questions and won students attention to those issues. The students became engaged in thinking through the problems, in confronting them, in looking at evidence and in reasoning rather than memorizing (Bain, 2004).

Biblical examples. There are several biblical examples that could be used to support the cause of mentorship and education; however, one of the greatest examples would be that of Paul and Timothy.

Paul and Timothy. One of the greatest relationships for mentorship was between Paul and Timothy. Some of the attributes that could be adopted were:

- Paul took Timothy under his tutelage and made the lessons personal
  o *"To Timothy, my beloved child: Grace, mercy, and peace from God the Father and Christ Jesus our Lord. I thank God whom I serve with a clear conscience, as did my fathers, when I remember you constantly in my prayers. As I remember your tears, I long night and day to see you that I may be filled with joy (II Timothy 1:2-4KJV).*
- He knew him personally as well as his lineage and life story

- o *I am reminded of your sincere faith, a faith that dwelt first in your grandmother Lois and your mother Eunice and now, I am sure, dwells in you (II Timothy 1:5).*
- ▪ He reminded him of his God given gifts
- o *Hence I remind you to rekindle the gift of God that is within you through the laying on of my hands; for God did not give us a spirit of timidity but a spirit of power and love and self-control" (II Timothy 1:6,7)*
- ▪ Paul reviewed what Timothy had learned through instruction and observation
- o *"Now you have observed my teaching, my conduct, my aim in life, my faith, my patience, my love, my steadfastness, my persecutions, my sufferings, what befell me at Antioch, at Iconium, and at Lystra, what persecutions I endured; yet from them all the Lord rescued me (II Timothy 3:10-11).*
- ▪ He warned him of the opposition to come

Indeed all who desire to live a godly life in Christ Jesus will be persecuted, while evil men and impostors will go on from bad to worse, deceivers and deceived. And he continually encouraged him. "But as for you, continue in what you have learned and have firmly believed, knowing from whom you learned it and how from childhood you have been acquainted with the sacred writings which are able to instruct you for salvation through faith in Christ Jesus" (II Timothy 3:12-15).

Theories of Christian Education

Divergent Theories Concerning Christian Education

There are two main points of divergent theories concerning Christian education that can be applied to the Christian education program that is mentioned here. They are divergent or differ in their approach as well as the expected outcome of their implementation (Klugman & Stump, 2006).

Critical Reasoning. The first divergent theory displays that a Christian education curriculum increases an individual's ability to reason critically when confronted with problems. This is done through the identification and analysis of problems and various outcomes. A Christian education curriculum would assist one in applying the biblical principles that they are taught to their everyday life occurrences (Klugman & Stump, 2006).

Manipulation of core values and traditions. The second divergent theory suggests that a Christian education curriculum is about the manipulating of core values and beliefs that may have been passed from generation to generation that may or may not echo truths as the Bible or religiosity speaks of (Klugman & Stump, 2006). This dispels the myths of the days of old that may have been passed from generation to generation with no biblical or moral truth or significance.

This provocation of thought would make one question as to whether teaching to a structured Christian education curriculum will change the students' beliefs and values. Given that the instructor helps them to remember what they knew before, would this act be beneficial or does such a course teach methods of reasoning so that students can make up their own minds (Klugman & Stump, 2006)?

Theoretical Frameworks

Maslow's Hierarchy of Needs

Maslow, who is considered the founder of humanistic psychology, proposed a theory of human motivation based on a hierarchy of needs. At the lowest level of his famous triangle hierarchy are physiological needs such as hunger and thirst, which must be attended to before one can deal with safety needs as well as those dealing with security and protection. The remaining levels are belonging and love, self-esteem, and finally, the need for self-actualization. This final need can be seen in a person's desire to become all that he or she is capable of becoming (Merriam, 2007).

For Maslow self-actualization is the goal of learning, and educators should strive to bring this about. Among the growth motivations were found the need for cognition, the desire to know and to understand. Learning is not only a form of psychotherapy but learning contributes to psychological health (Merriam, 2007). This theory is applicable to all learners in the fact that their attainment of the skill at hand is contingent upon the meeting the needs of the prior level of comfort. No matter the age or setting, if basic needs are not met then success cannot be expected. If there is no safety or security in the environment that secures the mindset of the individual then of course there will be an effect on academic attainment or retention and so on which means that of course self-actualization will not exist (Merriam, 2007).

Though the groups of learners will differ in their learning needs and processes, the diversification of implementation is still critical to their success. Such matters that need to be taken into consideration when designing learning strategies are age, background knowledge, outside elements such as home life and experience and how that plays a part in their learning experience as well.

The manner in which this framework lends itself into the effectiveness of this book is in the matter that there are prior needs that need to be addressed before expectations can be placed. If one encounters a homeless and hungry individual, then that basic physiological need must be met in order for the other levels of achievement to take place. The ultimate goal of the Christian Education experience that is spoken of is to assist members in experiencing that self-actualization level but the prior objectives must be met first.

Bronfenbrenner's Ecological Model

When there is no growth in the Pastor's personal life, no discipleship, few people in Bible Study then there is no mission or appropriate purpose for the church and there are no goals which means that there is nothing effective to be expected (Krejcir, 2007). The results of the above mentioned studies are that the Pastor must first and foremost be theologically sound. The bottom line is that Bible believing lay members want a pastor who tells of the truth of Christ, not one who waters down the word, nor one who preaches their inclinations, opinions, new ideas or the latest trends (Krejcir, 2007). This exercise in critical in the construction of a structured education program.

Educating the mind of individuals empowers their mind and renews their mindset. This truth echoes the expectations of the Apostle Paul that says, "And be not conformed to this world: but be ye transformed by the renewing of your mind, that ye may prove what is that good, and acceptable, and perfect, will of God (Romans 12:2, King James Version). The empowerment of education forces one to think outside of themselves. Bronfenbrenner's model depicts this statement.

Church attendance Patterns and Issues for Retention

Statistics bear witness on the stability of church attendance from 2011 to 2012 and the decline therein. Even the attendance in services is declining from 64% to 35%. The importance of religion declined from 79% to 20% which led to the decline in preference that went from 52.5 to 51.7% of the Christian population. These statistics are setting a trend for the demise of Christianity in relation to church membership and attendance (Newport, 2012).

There is a steady decline in the Protestant or other Christian religions over time from 2008 to the present and an increase in the" nones". When asked the question, "What are your religious preference-Protestant, Roman Catholic, Mormon, Jewish, Muslim, another religion, or no religion? In 2008 it was 14.6, in 2009 it was 15.3, in 2010 it was 16.4, in 2011 it was 17.5 and in 2012 it was a 17.8 (Newport, 2013). The answer "none" depicted includes the don't knows and those that refused to answer. Taking a deeper look at the dynamics of the "nones", would allow churches to know the audience that they should look for and target to attain membership.

The average congregation

Bruce (2004) gives statistics in reference to the average congregation. He completed a study that polled the congregation on several different questions like; why they attend services, what makes the services meaningful. He also addresses other preferences that worshippers have in reference to their worship experiences. Nearly 80% stated that they wanted effective Bible teaching.

Church Attendance

Many people attend religious services for several reasons. Many people go to church because they were always taught to go to church as an unspoken expectation but what was failed to be communicated is the relevance that religion has on the life that a person lives when they are religiously educated.

Church absences
When the Bible is taught in a real, effective and applicable way and the people still choose to leave, it often means they don't want to be challenged nor convicted among other reasons. (Krejcir, 2007). One of the top reasons people stop going to church is because of gossip and conflict. Healthy churches have a plan to recognize and then resolve sin and conflict. Churches that don't manage this behavior experience a decline in congregants and all that is left is hostility and only the creators of strife will stay while creating continuous chaos, factions, disunity, and strife (Krejcir, 2007).

Krejcir (2007) determined reasons and statistics for the church decline as a whole. This study is a product that was completed over a lengthy time frame of 12 years and shares some statistics about the occurrences that are taking place in the church today. Participants were asked a series of questions to the lay members as well as the leaders and compared the answers. After the survey was done an observational comparison study was made and the observers completed their own survey as well and reported its findings which included the health of the church, the connection to the church, biblical teaching, growth in Christ, it even asked how much time members were willing to invest in their faith development and what was most important to them about their church. These statistics gives some insight as to why churches fail.

Future Attendance Predictions

Half of the churches in the U.S. did not add any new members in the last two years (Krejcir, 2007). By 2025 attendance figures are assuming to drop to 15% and to 11 or 12% by 2050. Statistics state that 42-50% of all churches have a congregation of between 100-300 members with 20% having fewer than 100 (Krejcir, 2007).

Every year more than 4000 churches close their doors compared to the start of 1000 new church. There were about 15,000 new churches started between 1990 and 2000 with a 20% average of nearly 1000 per year. At the turn of last century (1900), there was a ratio of 27 churches per 10,000 people in America (Krejcir, 2007).

Given the ratios of closures of churches as compared to the new church starts, there should have been over 38,000 new churches commissioned to keep up with the population growth (Krejcir, 2007). These statistics should compel leaders to take action to make a great turn around.

In pursuit of creating a positive Christian experience for lay members and leadership, through this study, an encapsulation of the components of what a healthy and unhealthy church does and the attributes that they have been explored. Seeking to provide components to the religious edifice that will maintain former and attain new members is the objective of this study. From that desire, we are looking at the components that are said to be present in a healthy church.

According to Krejcir (2007) healthy churches;

- Have leaders who focus on Christ and serve Him;
- Have people that are disciplined and grow in Christ;
- Have a system of pastoral care;
- Have effective evangelism, stewardship, and discipleship;
- Are growing in Christ and have a well thought out, biblically empowered vision and mission statement;
- Tend to mobilize and organize their people according to their spiritual gifts
- Empower the people that are in their care;
- Are willing and do confront sin, evil, gossip, slander and manipulators and heresy in the church immediately;
- Have Pastors who are real, joyful, and authentic, and lead healthy, disciplined lives.

All of the above information that has been given serves a foundation and a data supported need to implement a Christian Education forum in every church. Bible study is great, Sunday school is good but a structured Christian education forum is vitally needed to ensure Christian living success. Now that the need has been established we can step into the meat and potatoes of this book, the 5 fold ministry gifts, their functions, what makes them vital and deal with the many misconceptions that are associated with them.

DIFFERENCES

Gift versus talent

Gift-

Something bestowed or acquired without any particular effort by the recipient or without being earned; a special ability or capacity; natural endowment

The bible dictionary states that gifts are bestowed freely by the holy spirit upon believers (James 1:17) for the edification of fellow believers and the church (Romans 1:11; 1 Corinthians 12:28)

James 1:17

17Every good gift and every perfect gift are from above, and cometh down from the Father of lights, with whom is no variableness, neither shadow of turning.

NOTE: many people interpret this scripture to mean that every good and perfect gift comes from heaven AND is heavenly to operate in. NOT SO! When one operates in their calling and does not waver in their convictions they often time become ridiculed and hated for the sake of the kingdom and IT DOES NOT FEEL GOOD! I have to urge you to remain true to your call even if it leaves you in the loneliest place on earth. Kingdom commitment hurts at times and don't let anyone tell you differently. There is always a level of persecution that comes with the call and it is vital that you allow your humanity to remain intact. Everyone may not be able to handle you when you are superpowerful under the influence of the anointing but super vulnerable in your humanity. They may call you a fake or phony but your humanity is what makes you authentic. It keeps you grounded and relatable in your efforts.

My personal practice is to try to surround myself with people who can handle the whole person that I am. I have a best friend that I have had for over 15 years and we live in two different cities and we don't even talk everyday but I know when I need to be completely human I can go to her without judgement and persecution. This is the great thing about having relationships with longevity because often times they can serve as sounding boards as well as gauges for your growth and development.

There is nothing worst than trying to talk humanity to what I call a "Spirit head" which are people who combat everything with scripture. Yes scripture can be applied to everything but not everytime. This goes back to our understanding of Maslow's Heirarchy of Needs.

Romans 1:11

11For I long to see you, that I may impart unto you some spiritual gift, to the end ye may be established;

Impartation is something that many get confused. The anointing is not like a common cold and cannot be passed in that manner. There is a difference between emulation, imitation and authentication.

A cubic zirconia is not a diamond though it looks like one and shines like one but when it comes to the authenticity and the value, this is where the difference is made. Unless one knows and understands this point they will put themselves in a position to be manipulated in a manner that will place them in bondage and leave them subject to being in open shame of the matters at hand.

I have seen pastors put babes up to minister before they are properly equipped and this is a dangerous practice due to the fact that they have no substance to them yet and no background knowledge. When this act is done it is good intention but bad idea. What happens in they leave the church for whatever reason, then they may go the new church and say, "I'm a minister, I have preached many times before in my old church!" then they are brought up to preach and left to an open shame. The intention was to boost their esteem but the idea is crucial and critical without proper explanation.

1 Corinthians 12:28

28And God hath set some in the church, first apostles, secondarily prophets, thirdly teachers, after that miracles, then gifts of healings, helps, governments, diversities of tongues.

Talent-

A special natural ability or aptitude:

The definitions just disclosed are vital to the process of discovery because many people feel that because they can do a thing means that is their gift or their calling and nothing can be further from the truth. For instance, I know people who have the ability to draw as a talent but they do not possess the gift. How do you know? You know it because it's something that they have to work at, whereas, if it was a gift, the ability comes without effort. For instance, I have never taken a voice lesson a day in my life but I can perform the riffs and runs that some megastars have learned through instruction so when they tell me to perform something by name I am clueless but once I see what they mean then I am able to perform the task effortlessly and achieve the same results as the learned individuals do. The reason is because I am gifted to sing and others are just talented. Now the pivotal point to understand is that though there is a great difference it does not make one superior over the other, in all actuality when paired correctly they actually complement each other. The only time it becomes a problem is when egos get in the way. Now we must understand that some people understand their gift but then some go and receive instruction on how to use their gift or operate in their calling and the office thereof. This is just an added benefit and is also a means of building credentials. For instance, some educators, such as myself, know that we are called to teach as well but I went to school to be earthly certified in man's eyes so that I could use this gift as a profession as well. But the acquisition of skills does not change the call or gift or the magnitude therein.

Called versus appointed

Called-

To command or request to come; summon

The bible dictionary defines a calling as the special summons to service which all Christians receive as a part of their salvation experience (1 Corinthians 7:20).

1 Corinthians 7:20

20Let every man abide in the same calling wherein he was called

The easiest way to remember this concept is that God calls but man appoints.

In many churches you see people walking around with various titles, which is fine, but their attitude and attributes is what will tell you whether they were called or appointed. In no way am I saying to confront people with this information but this information should sharpen your discernment on the matter and empower you to make a decision as to whether or not you want to follow individuals who were clearly appointed and not called or anointed in what they are doing.

The detriment to this is that man appoints people for various reasons and many of them may be for the wrong reason such as;

- Control-to keep the individual committed to that particular church
- Manipulation-in hopes to make the person more committed to the cause even though their hearts are far from it.
- Reward-some churches appoint people to positions as a way of rewarding their loyalty to the ministry which is clearly not a good reason nor rationale.

Note: To be appointed is fine but one must have the grace to stay in that position in the midst of opposition and this is where the rubber meets the road and many fail in the face of the people and are oftentimes left more damaged than effective.

There are also some good reasons that people are appointed to include;

- Elevation of faith-sometimes leadership (pastors and the like) see something in the individuals that they don't see in themselves and the leader is then held accountable to develop that gift for the sake of the kingdom. The problem with this is that they (leaders) appoint the individual and never develop the gift with knowledge of how to be effective in that gift or calling and so that leaves the individual to be ineffective and unsuccessful in their efforts which is a way of setting them up for failure.

Appointed versus Anointed

As discussed prior in the text,

Anointed is defined as the act of setting a person apart for a specific work or task. In the Old Testament times Kings, priests and prophets were anointed by having oil poured on their heads (Exodus 29:7)

Exodus 29:7

*7 Then shalt thou take the anointing oil, and
pour it upon his head, and anoint him*

All Christians are anointed for service in God's kingdom (2 Corinthians 1:21)

2 Corinthians 1:21

*21 Now he which stablisheth us with you in
Christ, and hath anointed us, is God;*

We have already talked about appointment by man but being anointed in an area is the greatest attribute one can possess. Anointing is when God has placed his stamp of approval on your life for usage by him. This is the optimal possession that one can have that comes with a guarantee for effectiveness and accurate usage.

DEFINITION

Office versus Operation

There is a distinct difference between operating in a gift and possessing/or walking in the office of the gift and the understanding of this principle is detrimental to the development of you as an individual as well as to the church. When one walks in the office that means that they are assigned by God to move in that sole calling only.

Romans 8:30

30Moreover whom he did predestinate, them he also called: and whom he called, them he also justified: and whom he justified, them he also glorified.

It does not mean that they can do nothing else but it does mean that this is their primary job. To be in the office means that you move in that calling no matter the location and your personality lines up with this office as well. Yes, all things in your being work together for the good of your gift.

<u>Romans 8:28</u>

*28And we know that all things work together for good to them that love God, to them who are **<u>the called</u>** according to his purpose*

We will get more into attributes later but just for the sake of an example, prophetic people are some of the loneliest people in the universe because no one understands them and when they try to partake in "normal conversation," people are always intimidated and read more into what they say so therefore they are people of few words because they understand the power and weight of the words that they speak.

Those who are apostolic thrive in order and structure and always see the bigger picture of any situation. They find the biblical reference in all current world events and do all that they can to remain relevant to the times and issues at hand.

Those who are called to the office of teaching are lifelong learners and thrive on the opportunity to learn as well as to teach are almost always effective in their efforts. I am more of the complex case because I am an avid learner, thus the many degrees but I absolutely love to teach and enlighten people on matter that they may not otherwise know.

These definitions will assist you in understanding the latter working of this book just know that there is a distinct difference between a calling to an office and the operation in a gift.

Calling

-The special Summation to service which all Christians receive as a part of their salvation experience.

<u>1 Corinthians 7:20-24</u>

20Let every man abide in the same calling wherein he was called.

21Art thou called being a servant? Care not for it: but if thou mayest be made free, use it rather.

22For he that is called in the Lord, being a servant, is the Lord's freeman: likewise also he that is called, being free, is Christ's servant.

23Ye are bought with a price; be not ye the servants of men.

24Brethren let every man, wherein he is called, therein abide with God.

<u>Anointing-</u>

The act of setting a person apart for a specific work or task. In Old Testament times kings, priests, and prophets were anointed by having oil poured on their heads

<u>Exodus 29:7</u>

7Then shalt thou take the anointing oil, and pour it upon his head, and anoint him.

Anointing for healing was practiced in New Testament times with the application of oil

<u>Mark 6:13</u>

13And they cast out many devils, and anointed with oil many that were sick, and healed them.

All Christians are anointed for service in God's Kingdom
<u>2Corinthians 1:21</u>

21Now he which stablisheth us with you in Christ, and hath anointed us, is God;

DEVELOPMENT

***No matter what the gift or calling etc.
is it has to be developed.***

Development means to bring out the capabilities or possibilities of; bring to a more advanced or effective state. In spiritual matters this piece is vitally important because people's spiritual well-beings are literally being entrusted into your hands. Sadly enough this is the one step that is left out of many churches and also why many are led astray and left hurt and humiliated.

Proverbs 18:21

*Death and life are in the power of the tongue: and
they that love it shall eat the fruit thereof.*

No matter which of the five-fold ministry gifts one possesses the power of their success and failure lies in their lifestyle and in their tongue. If one's lifestyle lacks character and integrity then people will have a hard time receiving them. So it is if you speak out of turn or out of season. This is why development of your gift is so crucial and it's not just about reading this book either, it is about finding and obtaining a covering that will formally teach you how to operate in your gift in that house. A great example is Elijah and Elisha. Their complete story is in the books of 1 and 2 Kings.

The key points that I want you to grasp from this story is

- How Elijah was instructed to anoint Elisha

1 Kings 19:16

And Jehu the son of Nimshi shalt thou anoint to be king over Israel: and Elisha the son of Shaphat of Abel—meholah shalt thou anoint to be prophet in thy room

- How and Why Elijah called him

1 Kings 19:19

So he departed thence, and found Elisha the son of Shaphat, who was plowing with twelve yoke of oxen before him, and he with the twelfth: and Elijah passed by him, and cast his mantle upon him.

- How and Why Elijah ministered to him

1 Kings 19:21

And he returned back from him, and took a yoke of oxen, and slew them, and boiled their flesh with the instruments of the oxen, and gave unto the people, and they did eat. Then he arose, and went after Elijah, and ministered unto him.

- The manner in which Elisha received the double portion of Elijah's spirit

<u>2 Kings 2:1-15</u>

1And it came to pass, when the Lord would take up Elijah into heaven by a whirlwind, which Elijah went with Elisha from Gilgal.

2And Elijah said unto Elisha, Tarry here, I pray thee; for the Lord hath sent me to Beth—el. And Elisha said unto him, As the Lord liveth, and as thy soul liveth, I will not leave thee. So they went down to Beth—el.

3And the sons of the prophets that were at Beth—el came forth to Elisha, and said unto him, Knowest thou that the Lord will take away thy master from thy head to day? And he said, Yea, I know it; hold ye your peace.

4And Elijah said unto him, Elisha, tarry here, I pray thee; for the Lord hath sent me to Jericho. And he said, As the Lord liveth, and as thy soul liveth, I will not leave thee. So they came to Jericho.

5And the sons of the prophets that were at Jericho came to Elisha, and said unto him, Knowest thou that the Lord will take away thy master from thy head to day? And he answered, Yea, I know it; hold ye your peace.

6And Elijah said unto him, Tarry, I pray thee, here; for the Lord hath sent me to Jordan. And he said, As the Lord liveth, and as thy soul liveth, I will not leave thee. And they two went on.

7And fifty men of the sons of the prophets went, and stood to view afar off: and they two stood by Jordan.

to view: Heb. in sight, or, over against

8And Elijah took his mantle, and wrapped it together, and smote the waters, and they were divided hither and thither, so that they two went over on dry ground.

9And it came to pass, when they were gone over, that Elijah said unto Elisha, Ask what I shall do for thee, before I be taken away from thee. And Elisha said, I pray thee, let a double portion of thy spirit be upon me.

10And he said, Thou hast asked a hard thing: nevertheless, if thou see me when I am taken from thee, it shall be so unto thee; but if not, it shall not be so.

Thou hast . . . : Heb. Thou hast done hard in asking

11And it came to pass, as they still went on, and talked, that, behold, there appeared a chariot of fire, and horses of fire, and parted them both asunder; and Elijah went up by a whirlwind into heaven.

12And Elisha saw it, and he cried, My father, my father, the chariot of Israel, and the horsemen thereof. And he saw him no more: and he took hold of his own clothes, and rent them in two pieces.

13He took up also the mantle of Elijah that fell from him, and went back, and stood by the bank of Jordan;

bank: Heb. lip

14And he took the mantle of Elijah that fell from him, and smote the waters, and said "Where is the Lord God of Elijah?" and when he also had smitten the waters, they parted hither and thither: and Elisha went over.

15And when the sons of the prophets which were to view at Jericho saw him, they said, The spirit of Elijah doth rest on Elisha. And they came to meet him, and bowed themselves to the ground before him.

2 Kings 3:11

11But Jehoshaphat said, Is there not here a prophet of the Lord that we may enquire of the Lord by him? And one of the kings of Israel's servants answered and said, "Here is Elisha the son of Shaphat, which poured water on the hands of Elijah."

This story in and of itself speaks volumes to this chapter and will summate my point in a very clear way. There are attributes that Elijah exhibited for Elisha and because of accumulation (of tutelage from Elijah) and association (with Elijah) Elisha was set up for success in his future ministry after the torch was passed down to him. There are some very vital lessons that are taught during the development phase.

Location (Education and Customs)

It is important to know that you are to operate in such a way in that house **ONLY** because every house is not the same. I may cook a meal one way for the members of my house but I may not be able to do the same thing at someone else's house because they may have food allergies or health issues and if I prepare the meal the same way without consulting the head of that household then I could literally kill someone.

1. *The building of self-confidence and God confidence*

The other reason that development is crucial is because when one is called to do a thing, a feeling of inadequacy almost immediately follows wherein they think of all the reasons why they should not perform the assigned task. It's okay it happens to the best of us;

Exodus 4:10

And Moses said unto the LORD, O my LORD, I am not eloquent, neither heretofore, nor since thou hast spoken unto thy servant: but I am slow of speech, and of a slow tongue.

2. *Word Acquisition* AND *Application*

Now you have to understand that development is not just the regurgitation of scriptures but the manifestation of scripture in your life. The devil even knows the scripture but look where it got him. I used to be amazed by people who can quote scripture off the top of their head but then I grew to understand head knowledge and heart knowledge. David said it best when he stated,

Psalm 119:11

*Thy word have I hid in mine heart, that
I might not sin against thee.*

Many people seek to impress others with the words that they remember and regurgitate. I remember as a young leader that I used to be impressed and moved by people who have the ability to quote scripture off the top of their head where I was one who had to go and research it to find it, though I knew it was there.

I found it fascinating but I found their application of those words more fascinating. I often think of the scripture that says to study to show thyself approved but then God revealed to me that some individuals study the words to prove themselves to be superior which is never a good move. Joshua said it best;

<u>Joshua 1:8</u>

This book of the law shall not depart out of thy mouth; but thou shalt meditate therein day and night, that thou mayest observe to DO according to all that is written therein: for then thou shalt make thy way prosperous, and then thou shalt have good success.

3. *Maturation*

A state of completion and fulfillment. Believers are urged to advance to mature teaching and "perfection" or fulfillment in good Works. The beautiful thing about maturation is that it happens over time and allows for us to see the development and growth of ourselves as well as others around us. Maturity is something that happens in spurts. There are things that my mother and others used to say to me as a kid that I never understood until I was older and then in an instant their words would come to me and make me think and understand their verbiage all at once. Another manner of maturity is when I encounter a situation at one point and then I turn around and encounter that issue again and handle it in a much more mature fashion that rings evident to my growth and maturity in the matter. Maturation in your calling happens in the same manner. For prophets, you learn that you don't always have to have a word for the people and you also learn how to receive a word. For the teachers, you learn the vitality and necessity of balance of teaching and learning. You never know it all and there is always something to learn. As a pastor, you learn the importance of networking and seeing how iron sharpens iron in the matter of ministry and how it functions.

Hebrews 6:1

1Therefore leaving the principles of the doctrine of Christ, let us go on unto perfection; not laying again the foundation of repentance from dead works, and of faith toward God,

2Of the doctrine of baptisms, and of laying on of hands, and of resurrection of the dead, and of eternal judgment.

3And this will we do, if God permit.

4For it is impossible for those who were once enlightened, and have tasted of the heavenly gift, and were made partakers of the Holy Ghost,

5And have tasted the good word of God, and the powers of the world to come,

6If they shall fall away, to renew them again unto repentance; seeing they crucify to themselves the Son of God afresh, and put him to an open shame.

While disclaiming perfection Paul urged believers to keep striving for perfection by being like Christ

Philippians 3:12-15

12Not as though I had already attained, either were already perfect: but I follow after, if that I may apprehend that for which also I am apprehended of Christ Jesus.

13Brethren, I count not myself to have apprehended: but this one thing I do, forgetting those things which are behind, and reaching forth unto those things which are before,

14I press toward the mark for the prize of the high calling of God in Christ Jesus.

15Let us therefore, as many as be perfect, be thus minded: and if in any thing ye be otherwise minded, God shall reveal even this unto you.

The revelation of this is that we should seek to complete the process for spiritual development

When the correct development takes place then manifestation becomes second nature. What many fail to realize is that personal devotion and study time is vital. Look at this rationale;

When you are in church on Sunday and the preacher is preaching, that is your point of education, they are imparting knowledge to you from the throne. The point of taking notes in church is for meditation and revelation during your time of personal devotion. After you have gone through the first two steps of the process then application of what you have learned should come easy for you. When the application portion is completed then evidence should be presented in the form of maturation and/or spiritual development. This means that you, as well as others, should see the difference in your behavior after having experienced the process. So it is with the gifts that we speak of.

Understand that all elements of the process are vital and cannot be omitted without impeding the development process.

All callings go through the same process:

Genesis of the Call

God told Jeremiah that he knew him before he was in his mother's womb this meant that before the breath of relief was taken by any party during the conception process, God had already spoken what he was going to be. Not only did he know what he was going to be, but he (God) knew the very DNA that would be necessary to partake in the Glory that would be revealed through the life and pain of the prophet and he ultimately equipped him with everything he needed for the journey. The recent revelation that God gave me in reference to the health issues that many leaders experience in their lives is often due to the fact that they are trying to do it (their ministry) in a manner other than the way in which God instructed them to do it bringing about additional stress and other related health issues and complications.

Many times we see leaders suffer from adverse health issues and oftentimes when we dig a little deeper we see that they are often guilty of;

- ➤ Trying to please the people and not so much God
- ➤ Trying to obtain possessions outside of their time and season
- ➤ Trying to move the hand of God with their own manipulative techniques

Adhering to the Genesis of the call is completely yielding your will to his and HONESTLY saying, "Lord, have YOUR way!" The problem is that few really mean it when they say it.

Birthing of the Call

Accepting the call within and moving strategically into that place.

The interesting thing about the birthing canal is that very rarely does anyone have to move the baby into position to be birthed; it is a natural progression that takes place. So it is in the spiritual realm! As God prepares his instruments for his ultimate use he positions them in places that they will forever be in. See when a baby is in the growing stages inside of the mother's womb the first thing that he or she hears is the heartbeat of his mother which is what we need to hear before taking the first step in any direction when it comes to ministry (the heartbeat of God). The interesting thing, even the more, is the position of the baby when he/she is preparing to come out and that is in a position of worship where the head is lower than the body. The spiritual is no different. When a baby comes out, they come out head first and after the head the first thing that most people look at are the eyes. What does this mean; it means that the vision is the first sense to manifest itself in the earth. YOU HAVE TO SEE BEFORE YOU CAN BE!

Pediatrics of the Call

Baby steps (small learning, large lessons) gifted in training

The first 18 years of life children go to their own pediatrician and milestones such as their height and weight are measured by these physicians who specialize in the health and maturation of the child. Leaders must hold themselves accountable to a covering that will measure their height and weight in the kingdom to gauge their ability to function. If you learn too much and never exercise the objectives you will become spiritually obese and unable to move at an adequate pace. If you move too much and too fast and are not feasting on the manna from heaven in the meantime, you will surely become spiritually anorexic and will surely die during delivery. Your spiritual pediatrician will hold you accountable but you must hold them accountable as well. They are to nurture and feed you as well as provide opportunities for you to walk out the instruction in which they have given you. Nothing is worse than a baby trying to walk, and their parents are encouraging them to do so but they (the child) are tied into a car seat and they are unable to move.

Wilderness of the Call

The wilderness is often called a place wherein you can't see the forest for the trees. What does this mean in Christendom? It means that the hurdles that stand in the way of my calling including myself (we can be our own worst enemy) prevent me from seeing the big picture of the office that I am called to.

*Perfecting of the gift and the understanding
of the logistics of the call.*

There are many logistics to the call and for everyone it is different but there are some logistics and questions that remain the same when one is trying to perfect their gift in a manner that is pleasing to God. Many begin with answering the five question words in relation to my call (who, what, when, where, how)!

Who-do I speak to?

What-do I say?

When-do I say it?

Where-in the service is it appropriate to speak?

How **(for the prophetic especially)**-do I tell them when the news is not as pleasant and bountiful as one would expect or how do I operate in my gifts when the people are unlearned?

As I encounter individuals from all over the world this is their biggest and most frequently asked questions, especially prophetic individuals. This is why the relationship and instruction that Elisha received from Elijah was so dynamic because not only was he able to study but I am sure his greatest lessons came through observation. We can speak all we want to but people are more prone to believe what they see versus what we say which is what makes living the life so critical. This is a great segue to our next developmental process . . .

Deep Water Call

> *Ministering the lessons of the wilderness, the basic and*
> *beyond totality of the foundational truth to people*
> *you don't know and who don't know you.*

Jesus told Peter to walk out on the water which was the execution of the faith that he had always been taught. This is the scariest place for every new leader, the execution of the lessons that you have been taught especially when you know that the teacher is always quiet during the test. The reason for their silence is to see the retention that you have of the material that you have been taught during the time of instruction and meditation. Being in ministry no matter which of the five-fold it is always about launching out into the deep and walking by faith. As we go through issues, we are always forced to exemplify the faith that we have learned and developed over time. This is what makes Christian development and/or faith development so vital because when operating in ministry it is all about the call and developing therein.

Matthew 15:22-33

22And straightway Jesus constrained his disciples to get into a ship, and to go before him unto the other side, while he sent the multitudes away.

23And when he had sent the multitudes away, he went up into a mountain apart to pray: and when the evening was come, he was there alone.

24But the ship was now in the midst of the sea, tossed with waves: for the wind was contrary.

25And in the fourth watch of the night Jesus went unto them, walking on the sea.

26And when the disciples saw him walking on the sea, they were troubled, saying, it is a spirit; and they cried out for fear.

27But straightway Jesus spake unto them, saying, Be of good cheer; it is I; be not afraid.

28And Peter answered him and said, Lord, if it be thou, bid me come unto thee on the water.

29And he said, Come. And when Peter was come down out of the ship, he walked on the water, to go to Jesus.

30But when he saw the wind boisterous, he was afraid; and beginning to sink, he cried, saying, Lord, save me.

31And immediately Jesus stretched forth his hand, and caught him, and said unto him, O thou of little faith, wherefore didst thou doubt?

32And when they were come into the ship, the wind ceased.

33Then they that were in the ship came and worshipped him, saying, Of a truth thou art the Son of God.

When faced with the fear and adversity, the natural reaction is the next developmental milestone;

Can I go back to my mother's womb?

The reaction to the ministerial persecution often results in spiritual regression, and the desire to go back to the birthing of the call. Can I find a hiding place perhaps go back to my mother's womb where I am neither seen nor heard but only exist? This part of the process is frequently visited no matter how long you have been walking in your calling. Change is something that people don't do well but yet the voice of God is continuously changing direction which means that the word that is delivered is one of change. Now if it's just human nature that people don't like change but the direction of implementation of God is forever changing, that implies that there may always be a struggle to get the people to adhere to the direction that God has for them to go in.

The are 7 C's to the ministerial call and these are the developmental stages of every leader that you must go through and it has to be sequential and move up because missing a step could become a future hurdle in your walk later;

The 7 C's of the Prophetic Calling

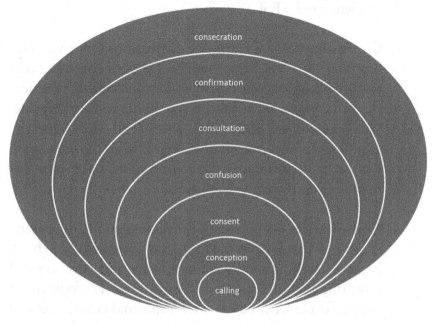

1. **Calling** (to command or request to come; summon)-God called you before you were in your mother's womb and not only did he call you but he also equipped you with everything that you need for the journey.

2. **Conception** (fertilization; inception of pregnancy)-he allowed the beauty of conception to take place between your mother and your father not because they were so in love but because they had the divine DNA to conceive the blessed gift . . . YOU!

3. **Consent**-(to permit, approve, or agree; comply or yield) God can call you all he wants but the contingency of the call is that you have to answer. Yes, he will keep knocking but only for a while then he has to take measures that will **MAKE** you answer, but remember our God is a gentleman and won't force himself on you or rape you of your will

but you do have to do something and that is give him a wholehearted YES!

4. **Confusion**-(lack of clarity or distinction) Once you give him the, "yes!" then there will be a state of confusion that you go through as you seek to understand what are the next steps that you need to take to stay in his will for your life. This book in itself will address part of this confusion stage as well as the next consultation stage. This is the stage when it is vitally important for you to find a mentor of some sort to guide you through the process.

5. **Consultation**-(a conference for discussion or the seeking of advice)-This is what the meat and potatoes of this book is about; seeking Godly counsel from your covering and acquiring literature that will assist in the development of your gift. Understanding what a spiritual covering is will be vital to your development and we will talk about what characteristics to look for when looking for a spiritual covering and these qualifications will be personally detrimental to your development and this will just be a starter list, there may be some things that you think of that you need to add to the list that will make you feel more comfortable and make that person more qualified to cover you in that manner. One thing that is critical to understand in this process is the term "covering." Many people confuse "covering" with "controlling" and they are completely opposite terms. When one covers you, that means that they have lended themselves to be as a mentor to you, to guide you and to protect you. When it comes to them telling what you can and cannot do, flags should appear as a means of caution. Not that they won't ever tell you that they don't think that you can do this or that for developmental reasons but they should be able to biblically tell you the rationale for their decision. At the end of the day you owe them nothing but a thank you. When it gets

to the point that they speak of a debt that you owe them for their services it is time to clearly move around and find a more authentic mentor. For instance, at one time I attended a church wherein I was over the praise and worship team and I also was a prophetic voice in the house as well as a teacher. I always make it a point to ensure that my leaders understand that I travel excessively and may not always be available. When an opportunity came and I had to be out the leader threatened to sit me down and not let me be active if I didn't show up to his event. This, my friend, is control. Had he said, "Jennifer, I think it would be really beneficial for you to stay here and attend this event because it will do XYZ for your gifting and development." That presentation is a lot less intrusive and controlling. This is what I mean about the controlling caution flags.

6. **Confirmation**-(made certain as to truth, accuracy, validity, availability) After hearing from everything and everyone else, you have to then turn your face to the wall as Hezekiah did and seek confirmation and revelation of what parts God wants you to keep or even better what he wants you to purge. Every part of what you read and hear is not for you to keep and utilize some things God will just allow you to encounter for the purpose of identification and not for implementation in your own walk.

<u>2 Kings 20:1-6</u>

those days was Hezekiah sick unto death. And the prophet Isaiah the son of Amoz came to him, and said unto him, Thus saith the Lord, Set thine house in order; for thou shalt die, and not live.

2Then he turned his face to the wall, and prayed unto the Lord, saying,

3I beseech thee, O Lord, remember now how I have walked before thee in truth and with a perfect heart, and have done that which is good in thy sight. And Hezekiah wept sore.

4And it came to pass, afore Isaiah was gone out into the middle court, that the word of the Lord came to him, saying,

5Turn again, and tell Hezekiah the captain of my people, Thus saith the Lord, the God of David thy father, I have heard thy prayer, I have seen thy tears: behold, I will heal thee: on the third day thou shalt go up unto the house of the Lord.

6And I will add unto thy days fifteen years; and I will deliver thee and this city out of the hand of the king of Assyria; and I will defend this city for mine own sake, and for my servant David's sake.

7. **Consecration**-(dedication to the service and worship of a deity) this final process is ongoing as are the other processes but this one is major because you have to stay in a place of consecration for the duration of the utilization of your ministry in the faith. This is the only way to stay fine-tuned for Kingdom and make sure that you are hearing what God is saying not what he SAID, like Abraham when it came to slaying his promised seed. He heard what the spirit of God said when he told him to go and take Isaac and slay him but what spared Isaac's life is that his father stayed in tune with the voice of God when he told him to stead thy hand which spared the very life of his son! Consecration keeps one relevant, sane and competent for Kingdom use.

Genesis 22:1-18

1And it came to pass after these things that God did tempt Abraham, and said unto him, Abraham: and he said, Behold, here I am.

2And he said, Take now thy son, thine only son Isaac, whom thou lovest, and get thee into the land of Moriah; and offer him there for a burnt offering upon one of the mountains which I will tell thee of.

3And Abraham rose up early in the morning, and saddled his ass, and took two of his young men with him, and Isaac his son, and clave the wood for the burnt offering, and rose up, and went unto the place of which God had told him.

4Then on the third day Abraham lifted up his eyes, and saw the place afar off.

5And Abraham said unto his young men, Abide ye here with the ass; and I and the lad will go yonder and worship, and come again to you.

6And Abraham took the wood of the burnt offering, and laid it upon Isaac his son; and he took the fire in his hand, and a knife; and they went both of them together.

7And Isaac spake unto Abraham his father, and said, My father: and he said, Here am I, my son. And he said, Behold the fire and the wood: but where is the lamb for a burnt offering?

8And Abraham said, My son, God will provide himself a lamb for a burnt offering: so they went both of them together.

9And they came to the place which God had told him of; and Abraham built an altar there, and laid the wood in order, and bound Isaac his son, and laid him on the altar upon the wood.

10And Abraham stretched forth his hand, and took the knife to slay his son.

11And the angel of the Lord called unto him out of heaven, and said, Abraham, Abraham: and he said, Here am I.

12And he said, Lay not thine hand upon the lad, neither do thou any thing unto him: for now I know that thou fearest God, seeing thou hast not withheld thy son, thine only son from me.

13And Abraham lifted up his eyes, and looked, and behold behind him a ram caught in a thicket by his horns: and Abraham went and took the ram, and offered him up for a burnt offering in the stead of his son.

14And Abraham called the name of that place Jehovah—jireh: as it is said to this day, In the mount of the Lord it shall be seen

15And the angel of the Lord called unto Abraham out of heaven the second time,

16And said, By myself have I sworn, saith the Lord, for because thou hast done this thing, and hast not withheld thy son, thine only son:

17That in blessing I will bless thee, and in multiplying I will multiply thy seed as the stars of the heaven, and as the sand which is upon the sea shore; and thy seed shall possess the gate of his enemies

18And in thy seed shall all the nations of the earth be blessed; because thou hast obeyed my voice.

All of these steps are continual but the initial utilization of them has to be sequential.

DETACHMENT

To detach is to unfasten and separate; disengage; disunite.

In my book, "And Deliver Us from People: The Revelation for Elevation" I discuss the importance of being delivered and sometimes detached from people in your life. Well, as you develop in your gifting you will also encounter a detachment period that is bound to happen and in some instances is vital for your success. During your development God will strengthen and prepare you for this period of desertion but you have to be able to hear his voice. There are times when there will be others around you that will try to be louder than the voice of God with their opinions and perceptions of things. God will not allow this disturbance to happen because he is focused on your purpose and not your pursuit of a personal relationship with others.

2 Corinthians 6:14-18

14Be ye not unequally yoked together with unbelievers: for what fellowship hath righteousness with unrighteousness? and what communion hath light with darkness?

15And what concord hath Christ with Belial? or what part hath he that believeth with an infidel?

16And what agreement hath the temple of God with idols? for ye are the temple of the living God; as God hath said, I will dwell in them, and walk in them; and I will be their God, and they shall be my people.

17Wherefore come out from among them, and be ye separate, saith the Lord, and touch not the unclean thing; and I will receive you,

18And will be a Father unto you, and ye shall be my sons and daughters, saith the Lord Almighty.

See the diagram below from my book, "And Deliver Us from People"

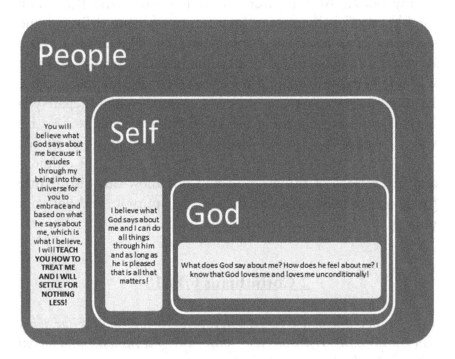

God is the only individual that you have to seek confirmation from . . . look at this analogy a little deeper from the last chapter . . .

Confirmation-(made certain as to truth, accuracy, validity, availability) After hearing from everything and everyone else, you have to then turn your face to the wall as Hezekiah did and seek confirmation and revelation of what parts God wants you to keep or even better what he wants you to purge. Every part of what you read and hear is not for you to keep and utilize some things God will just allow you to encounter for the purpose of identification and not for implementation in your own walk.

When I was working on my Bachelors in education to be a teacher in the secular world, I remember one of my professors saying that everyone should make a "Wanna Do" and "Don't Wanna Do" list as we encounter different teachers and professionals in the teacher's program. I took this concept and integrated into my personal life as well. There are seasons where I go to different churches and I wonder why I am there and when I walk away from that season with that church I make some deep reflections of that experience and I add to either one, if not both, of these lists and keep it close and handy to me even if it is in my mind. I remember things like

- How it made me feel when they_____.
- What was the reaction that I saw in the people as this rule or bylaw was implemented or discussed.

These are just a few of the matters that I consider when I encounter people on a day to day basis. This does several things for me;

- Keeps me humble-realizing that I too make mistakes
- Keeps me from idolizing other people-realizing, that at any given moment man is apt to fall and/or make a bad choice
- Keeps me learning-as I see my lists growing or I begin to share experiences that I have seen or heard or even read about then I know that this experience as well as the others are only going to make me greater later.

61

Please know that there are going to be people in your life that God will attach and detach you to for the sake of the Kingdom, very few people are in your life to stay and the sooner, you understand that the less painful the detachment process will be. This is also where the spiritual covering is important but you have to be careful who you call your spiritual covering.

Spiritual Covering

When I speak of a spiritual covering, I speak of one who will hold you accountable for your gifts and calling as well as your lifestyle. (YES YOUR LIFESTYLE!) I had to make sure that I stress that because a true spiritual covering will not allow you to segment your life by monitoring this facet of your life but not that one. Here are just a few things that you want and don't want in a spiritual covering.

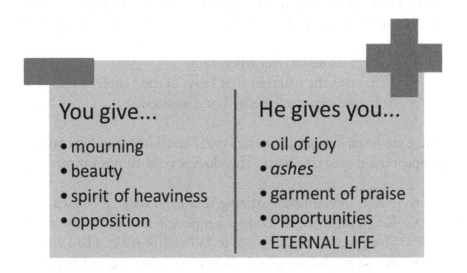

You give...	He gives you...
• mourning	• oil of joy
• beauty	• *ashes*
• spirit of heaviness	• garment of praise
• opposition	• opportunities
	• ETERNAL LIFE

There are many other attributes that I can mention but for the sake of time and space I would like it if you added to your own list that is provided to you in the appendix of this book. There are things that one person may need that another may not see as important.

Something else that I think is worth looking at and comparing this list to are the attributes that Elijah exemplified as he mentored Elisha. (1 Kings 19)

Detour

Many of us have our lives planned out and a vision for ourselves but the hardest part of being called to kingdom is the fact that you have to be flexible and be able to detour from what your personal plans and aspirations are and be ready and willing to follow the father and his plans for your life. I am certain that it wasn't easy for the disciples as they were instructed to lay down their livelihoods to follow the father.

When you read the charge of the disciples in Matthew Chapter 10. There was a lot of responsibility given to them. Many people see the glory of the works that they completed but they never look at the story.

Matthew 10

1And when he had called unto him his twelve disciples, he gave them power against unclean spirits, to cast them out, and to heal all manner of sickness and all manner of disease.

2Now the names of the twelve apostles are these; The first, Simon, who is called Peter, and Andrew his brother; James the son of Zebedee, and John his brother;

3Philip, and Bartholomew; Thomas, and Matthew the publican; James the son of Alphaeus, and Lebbaeus, whose surname was Thaddaeus;

4Simon the Canaanite, and Judas Iscariot, who also betrayed him.

5These twelve Jesus sent forth, and commanded them, saying, Go not into the way of the Gentiles, and into any city of the Samaritans enter ye not:

6But go rather to the lost sheep of the house of Israel.

7And as ye go, preach, saying, The kingdom of heaven is at hand.

8Heal the sick, cleanse the lepers, raise the dead, cast out devils: freely ye have received, freely give.

9Provide neither gold, nor silver, nor brass in your purses,

10Nor scrip for your journey, neither two coats, neither shoes, nor yet staves: for the workman is worthy of his meat.

11And into whatsoever city or town ye shall enter, enquire who in it is worthy; and there abide till ye go thence.

12And when ye come into an house, salute it.

13And if the house be worthy, let your peace come upon it: but if it be not worthy, let your peace return to you.

14And whosoever shall not receive you, nor hear your words, when ye depart out of that house or city, shake off the dust of your feet.

15Verily I say unto you, It shall be more tolerable for the land of Sodom and Gomorrha in the day of judgment, than for that city.

16Behold, I send you forth as sheep in the midst of wolves: be ye therefore wise as serpents, and harmless as doves.

17But beware of men: for they will deliver you up to the councils, and they will scourge you in their synagogues;

18And ye shall be brought before governors and kings for my sake, for a testimony against them and the Gentiles.

19But when they deliver you up, take no thought how or what ye shall speak: for it shall be given you in that same hour what ye shall speak.

20For it is not ye that speak, but the Spirit of your Father which speaketh in you.

21And the brother shall deliver up the brother to death, and the father the child: and the children shall rise up against their parents, and cause them to be put to death.

22And ye shall be hated of all men for my name's sake: but he that endureth to the end shall be saved.

23But when they persecute you in this city, flee ye into another: for verily I say unto you, Ye shall not have gone over the cities of Israel, till the Son of man be come.

24The disciple is not above his master, nor the servant above his lord.

25It is enough for the disciple that he be as his master, and the servant as his lord. If they have called the master of the house Beelzebub, how much more shall they call them of his household?

26Fear them not therefore: for there is nothing covered, that shall not be revealed; and hid, that shall not be known.

27What I tell you in darkness, that speak ye in light: and what ye hear in the ear, that preach ye upon the housetops.

28And fear not them which kill the body, but are not able to kill the soul: but rather fear him which is able to destroy both soul and body in hell.

29Are not two sparrows sold for a farthing? and one of them shall not fall on the ground without your Father.

30But the very hairs of your head are all numbered.

31Fear ye not therefore, ye are of more value than many sparrows.

32Whosoever therefore shall confess me before men, him will I confess also before my Father which is in heaven.

33But whosoever shall deny me before men, him will I also deny before my Father which is in heaven.

34Think not that I am come to send peace on earth: I came not to send peace, but a sword.

35For I am come to set a man at variance against his father, and the daughter against her mother, and the daughter in law against her mother in law.

36And a man's foes shall be they of his own household.

37He that loveth father or mother more than me is not worthy of me: and he that loveth son or daughter more than me is not worthy of me.

38And he that taketh not his cross, and followeth after me, is not worthy of me.

39He that findeth his life shall lose it: and he that loseth his life for my sake shall find it.

40He that receiveth you receiveth me, and he that receiveth me receiveth him that sent me.

41He that receiveth a prophet in the name of a prophet shall receive a prophet's reward; and he that receiveth a righteous man in the name of a righteous man shall receive a righteous man's reward.

42And whosoever shall give to drink unto one of these little ones a cup of cold water only in the name of a disciple, verily I say unto you, he shall in no wise lose his reward.

What my remains for you, is that you will see the big picture of your calling and understand that it is not about you but about the assignment that you were given at the time of your call. We find ourselves singing, "I Surrender All" but forget "all" includes some things and/or people whom you may hold dear to you. This (the detour) is one of the hardest objectives for anyone to meet. Even people who lack a solid vision for their life don't want to be susceptible to the plan of God because often times it involves doing something that you clearly don't want to do. There should be comfort in the fact that Jesus done the same thing . . . remember when he said, take this cup from me . . .

Matthew 26:39

And he went a little further, and fell on his face, and prayed, saying, O my Father, if it be possible, let this cup pass from me: nevertheless not as I will, but as thou wilt.

This was a clear example of his humanity but yet and still he continued to be about the father's business and continued on the path that was laid for him. One of the most difficult parts of being gifted, called and anointed is yielding your will to the will of the father. Sure you can always go against the grain and do what you want to do but you have to understand that there will be consequences to every action that you choose. Many times I wonder if the gift of free choice that God gives us is actually a gift or a curse. It's like giving an irresponsible 18 year old a million dollars; it could be the catalyst to reckless endangerment. Though there is no fix for this reality of the detours in life, please take comfort in the reality of the human emotions that you feel knowing that you are not alone.

Mark 10:28-31

28Then Peter began to say unto him, Lo, we have left all, and have followed thee.

29And Jesus answered and said, Verily I say unto you, There is no man that hath left house, or brethren, or sisters, or father, or mother, or wife, or children, or lands, for my sake, and the gospel's,

30But he shall receive an hundredfold now in this time, houses, and brethren, and sisters, and mothers, and children, and lands, with persecutions; and in the world to come eternal life.

31But many that are first shall be last; and the last first.

For many the above scripture is a happy ending because it promises that the last will be first and it also holds a host of promises from God but the one word that we often overlook in the achieving and receiving the promises of God is the one word that is the hardest to overcome at times and this the word "persecution." How you handle the obstacles in life is oftentimes also how you will handle the opportunities in life. That is why no matter what the obstacles are you have to face it with this understanding,

Philippians 1:6

6Being confident of this very thing, that he which hath begun a good work in you will perform it until the day of Jesus Christ:

I guarantee that you will face obstacles in your life especially when you give God a wholehearted "yes." But no matter what remember;

<u>Isaiah 61:1-4</u>

1The Spirit of the Lord God is upon me; because the Lord hath anointed me to preach good tidings unto the meek; he hath sent me to bind up the brokenhearted, to proclaim liberty to the captives, and the opening of the prison to them that are bound;

2To proclaim the acceptable year of the Lord, and the day of vengeance of our God; to comfort all that mourn;

3To appoint unto them that mourn in Zion, to give unto them beauty for ashes, the oil of joy for mourning, the garment of praise for the spirit of heaviness; that they might be called trees of righteousness, the planting of the Lord, that he might be glorified.

4And they shall build the old wastes, they shall raise up the former desolations, and they shall repair the waste cities, the desolations of many generations.

Remember that Christ has called you to assist in the facilitation of what I like to call, "The Great Exchange."

DETOX

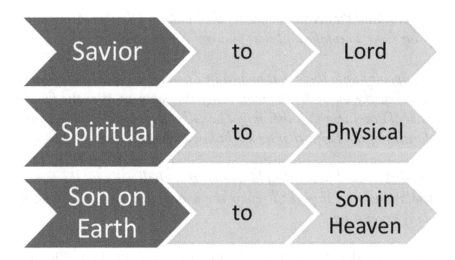

Isaiah 61:3

3To appoint unto them that mourn in Zion, to give unto them beauty for ashes, the oil of joy for mourning, the garment of praise for the spirit of heaviness; that they might be called trees of righteousness, the planting of the Lord, that he might be glorified.

Detox is the most painful part of the process because it is where you are often led to the sifter that purges matters and members of your life, even the ones or the things that you love the most.

This is the place where you are able to decipher the difference between your will and the fathers will. Whenever you encounter a recovered addict of any sort the first thing that they tell you in reference to their recovery is that detox was the hardest part. So it is in the kingdom. Our own will is often our drug of choice and our consistent high and when we finally yield our will then we experience some pains and discomforts that we know are for our benefit but does not take away the fact that there is a high level of discomfort.

You have to realize that many people die during the detoxification process. Detox can create a number of symptoms in your body as your body goes through the process of purifying itself and eliminating toxins. Some common earthly detox symptoms include:

- Headaches
- lethargy (drowsiness)
- temporary muscle aches
- mucus or other discharge
- a coated, pasty tongue
- flu-like symptoms
- irritability
- difficulty sleeping
- weakness
- cravings
- nausea

Medical doctors say that you may even find that the detoxing process causes you to suffer the old symptoms that you have had that the body had suppressed. They say that you may think that you are becoming ill but it is important that you continue with the detox and don't take any medications to help with the symptoms. The aim is to flush chemicals from the body, not introduce more!

You have to understand the spiritual detoxification is the same way. It is very uncomfortable and you will experience some of the same symptoms of the natural detoxification process. The difference is the rationale or reasons for those symptoms are different. For example;

Headaches-comes from trying to think your way out of your destiny in ministry

Lethargy (drowsiness)-comes from trying to out run the will of the father (impossible)

Temporary muscle aches-comes from fighting against the will of God

Mucus or other discharge-comes from what many call purging during warfare which is the manifestation of the effectiveness of warfare and the excretion of matter that needs to be eliminated in order to clearly walk in your calling and purpose.

A coated, pasty tongue-comes from the need to change the language that one speaks over their lives and destiny. There is a need to speak about the matter the way that the father speaks so that those words can be manifested.

Flu-like symptoms-comes from the discomfort of your members being forced to line up with the will of God.

Irritability-comes from the understanding that there is always a level of agitation when there is a battle of the wills (between what you want to do and what God wants you to do.). This symptom has to definitely be understood by the leadership and covering and understanding that when the irritability takes over and the manifestation is the lashing that many people do, don't take it personal but understand it is a spiritual battle.

Difficulty sleeping-there are times when the spirit of God will not allow one to rest in their current status and state. You may be able to sleep a bit but you won't get good rest because you are still warring in your spirit man.

Weakness-I am known for preaching and speaking about the frailty of my humanity. I am the first one to speak on how I am so glad that I serve the God of another chance because of the MANY times I fall and get up but the weakness comes moreso in the times when I throw myself down because I don't want to live right. This is the message that people really need to hear because too often they are left thinking that we as believers have it all together and that they cannot come to Christ until they also "get it all together" we have to be transparent enough to let them know that daily we have to die to our flesh. David said it best when he stated,

Romans 7:14-25

14For we know that the law is spiritual: but I am carnal, sold under sin.

15For that which I do I allow not: for what I would, that do I not; but what I hate, that do I.

16If then I do that which I would not, I consent unto the law that it is good.

17Now then it is no more I that do it, but sin that dwelleth in me.

18For I know that in me (that is, in my flesh,) dwelleth no good thing: for to will is present with me; but how to perform that which is good I find not.

19For the good that I would I do not: but the evil which I would not, that I do.

20Now if I do that I would not, it is no more I that do it, but sin that dwelleth in me.

21I find then a law, that, when I would do good, evil is present with me.

22For I delight in the law of God after the inward man:

23But I see another law in my members, warring against the law of my mind, and bringing me into captivity to the law of sin which is in my members.

24O wretched man that I am! who shall deliver me from the body of this death?

25I thank God through Jesus Christ our Lord. So then with the mind I myself serve the law of God; but with the flesh the law of sin.

Cravings-this same scripture can be used for this symptom because it comes from dealing with the desire to continue in the error of your ways.

Nausea-comes during the spiritual detoxification process there will be times when the sin that you once were guilty of partaking in will make you nauseous. This takes place when the time comes and the manifestation is closer than the appearance.

You may even find that the detoxing process causes you to suffer the old symptoms and the sins of your past will look appealing oftentimes because you have only suppressed it versus dealing with it. You may think that you are becoming ill or backsliding and you may fall into the lap of temptation but it is important that you continue with the detox and don't take any medications nor fall into the "woe is me syndrome" to help with the symptoms, dust yourself off and move on. This is where grace and mercy come in and why we should be grateful that it is anew every morning. The aim is to flush the sin from the body, not introduce more nor wallow in your mistakes!

DETERMINATION

There is not a single most critical piece of the five-fold ministry. When you are truly called the first thing that comes into your head is, "Do I really have what it takes to carry this mantle." The answer is yes! Everything that you need God placed in you before your parents tagged you with a name, as a matter of fact before your parents ever met. God told Jeremiah that he knew him before he was in his mother's womb this meant that before the breath of relief was taken by any party during the conception process, God had already spoken what he was going to be. Not only did he know what he was going to be but he (God) knew the very DNA that would be necessary to partake in the Glory that would be revealed through the life and pain of the prophet and he ultimately equipped him with everything he needed for the journey. This is where the beginning of the call began and everything else that happened during the furtherance of your journey was just building blocks or shall we say hurdles that were used to establish your balance for the kingdom.

There is a continuum that takes place in your journey to make sure that you remain balanced when life throws hurdles in your path. See when a runner competes in a race the main components that they must have is not just speed but pace and balance. They were not born fast as one would think but the inner working that they needed to develop that speed was placed in them at birth but developed throughout the stages of their life.

The dictionary defines a son as a person related as if by ties of sonship. That is the natural definition. The Spiritual revelatory definition for the sake of this chapter is the fact that I have;

- transferred my thinking,
- transfigured my ways and
- Transcended my own beliefs of what it is that I can really do.

That means that my relationship with Christ has changed from Savior (a person who saves, rescues, or delivers) to Lord (a person who has power and authority over me). My walk begins in the spiritual and is manifested in the physical and due to my complete submission and obedience, I understand that not only am I am son on Earth but due to my complete surrender I will be a son in Heaven as well.

THE TWELVE COMMANDMENTS OF SONSHIP

What it means to truly be a son means

1. I will not forget what the father has called me to be

2. Despite what others think, I will walk in my conviction or leading of the Holy Ghost

3. I will not allow my anointing to be prostituted in any manner by any man

4. I will embrace the rights of the father to change his mind which means that I have the right to change my prophesy and understand it does not make me any less anointed

5. I will not be discouraged when I am not honored in my home or received by my own kind because the bible tells me that a prophet is never honored in their own home anyway. (Matthew 13:57)

6. I will remain mature (a meat eater), not return to milk as a babes do, and will walk in the mystery of Christ (remaining on the cutting edge and relevance of scripture)

7. I will remain secure in my calling, come what may, and understand to be a son means to live a life of integrity and faithfulness to my call and to Christ as well as to the body.

8. I will not become jealous of my siblings realizing that we all may have the same father but different anointing as well as different degrees of anointing.

9. I will not be offended when my anointing is not called upon for usage at a certain time, but I will realize that every assembly is not meant for me to speak or participate.

10. I will celebrate the usage of the other gifts and callings but will not be fearful to hold them accountable under the conviction of the Holy Ghost.

11. I commit to maintaining a heart and mindset of repentance at all costs for the edification of the Kingdom and the continual killing of my flesh and will live my lifestyle accordingly.

12. I will remain humble in my calling realizing that it is Christ, not me, and it is for the building and edification of his kingdom and not my own.

ACTIVATION

The final stage that one partakes in is the activation phase where in you have been equipped with knowledge and know how to effectively implement and walk in your calling. This includes having the ability to answer the five question words in reference to your call by;

The perfecting (maturing) of the gift and the understanding of the logistics of the call.

Answering the five question words in relation to my call (who, what, when, where, how)!

Who-do I speak to?

What-do I say?

When-do I say it?

Where-in the service is it appropriate to speak?

How **(for the prophetic especially)**-do I tell them when the news is not as pleasant and bountiful as one would expect or how do I operate in my gifts when the people are unlearned?

JUST REMEMBER WHENEVER YOU ARE IN DOUBT

!!!!PRAY!!!!

1 Thessalonians 5:17

says Pray without ceasing.

Ready? Set? Go . . .

Now to the Five-fold
Ministry Gifts

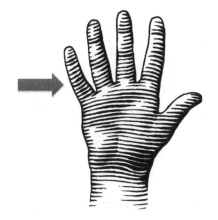

Teacher

TEACHER

What is it?

A person who communicates knowledge or religious truth to others. Persons whose skill and ministry are vital to the church (Ephesians 4:11-12)

Where are they located? Significance?

These individuals are the foundation of the hand. The smallest finger but makes the largest impact in the body. Teachers are one of the ones who are an absolute necessity because they set the individuals up for success. They are also at times closest to the leadership such as the Pastor and Apostle because they help to convey the basic foundation of the word and they help to establish foundational order.

Personal Attributes-

Inquisitive, a natural researcher of facts (even random thoughts)

Who are some in the Bible?

Master and teacher are used interchangeably in the Bible and were often applied to Christ (Matthew 22:16)

Samuel (Head of the school of the prophets 1Samuel 19:20)

Elisha (Head at Gilgal 2 Kings 4:38)

When should a new convert encounter them?

A new convert should encounter the teacher right after a brief consultation with the Pastor. The Pastor then passes the individual off to the teacher for tutelage. The beginning point for every teacher is the plan of salvation and explaining what that is. Then insistence upon the individual attending church, Bible study and school should take place.

Weekly touchups should take place as the individual begins to attend the learning opportunities to make sure that they are understanding what is going on and not lost in the shuffle of instruction. Many times, in ministry, we just assume that people know what we are talking about because we are talking about it. You will often hear preachers say phrases like, "You know the story of . . ." or "Remember . . ." and some people get caught up in the moment and holler "Yeah" and miss the gist of what was said because they were ignorant to the background information (all of us as ministers are guilty of this). This is why it is always important to give a brief synopsis of the story that you are referencing or to give a little background knowledge so that all of the people can keep up with you and enjoy the journey that you are taking them on.

How do they generally operate?

Teachers generally operate in a manner in which they find themselves explaining occurrences that happen and they often have a deeper understanding for the context in which a word is spoken. If you remember when Jesus taught, he taught them according to their profession or back ground knowledge. For fisherman he talked their language, for carpenters, he taught their language etc. Teachers are great generators of creative ideas for getting concepts across. If they are really good, they also provide opportunities for knowledge that the trainee has attained to be tested either through a paper-pencil test or a test of application. These assessments should be fun and exciting for all parties involved but most of all they should be backed by the word of God. This is the most vital part of this calling is that this individual is astute in the word of God to ensure that every word, thought or concept that they introduce is backed by the word of God and not their opinion.

Teaching is more than just a transmission experience where they teacher talks and the student listens. When scripture is quoted, the address of that scripture should also be disclosed to allow the students themselves to study the word and build a topical memory system of frequently used scriptures. Teachers should also be a resource that students are able to use when they want to know certain things about the bible. They should also be able to recommend certain books for certain issues that will be more applicable to the situation that the individual may be going through. In the appendix there is a resource called the Topical Memory System that I always share with new and old converts to help to build them up in their most holy faith and their spiritual confidence. This is list of the most commonly used scriptures and their addresses in the bible to just start the students on their journey to having a heart full of word and there are so many ways that one can allow opportunities for individuals to recite these scriptures and commit them to their memory banks for later usage.

See the topical memory system in the appendix

Why are they so vital to the Body of Christ?

Teachers are vital to the body for so many reasons but mainly because they, like the prophets who we will get to later are the ones who can take the occurences in the church and reference it to an occurrence in the Bible and make all of it applicable to each other.

The teacher is the conductor to this process. It all comes from them to go back to them. They provide the education and the educational opportunities for the students and then they show them the need and vitality of meditation and revelation which is the fruits of a personal relationship as well as personal study and devotion time and tells them how to implement it and then they watch the student in their walk to see if the application in their lives is evident.

Qualifications of a teacher

- Must be patient
- Must be knowledgeable of the word
- Must be flexible and creative in their educational approach
- Must be personable and not threatening

PASTOR

PASTOR

<u>*What is it?*</u>

One who leads and instructs a congregation.

Jeremiah 3:15

And I will give you pastors according to mine heart, which shall feed you with knowledge and understanding.

Called to God to perfect the saints and buildup the body of Christ

Ephesians 4:11-13

11And he gave some, apostles; and some, prophets; and some, evangelists; and some, pastors and teachers; 12For the perfecting of the saints, for the work of the ministry, for the edifying of the body of Christ: 13Till we all come in the unity of the faith, and of the knowledge of the Son of God, unto a perfect man, unto the measure of the stature of the fullness of Christ:

Where are they located? Significance? The Pastor is the ring finger on the hand because he is married spiritually to the church. Now this has to be said with a word of caution because if he is married earthly to a spouse it can at times cause a conflict unless the spouse is a kingdom worker as well and even in that, there has to be balance in the relationship both spiritually and earthly.

Personal Attributes

Pastors are nearly and most often a natural born leader, one to set order and delegates authority in the local setting under the direction of the Holy Ghost.

Who are some in the Bible?

Pastors were often referred to as shepherds in the Bible
Abel (Genesis 4:2)
*Rachel (Genesis 29:9)
*The daughters of Jethro (Exodus 2:16)
Moses (Exodus 3:1)
David (2 Samuel 7:8)

* This should do away with the belief that women cannot be Pastors because look at how many were in the Bible and this just names a few.

When should a new convert encounter them?

Once the evangelist brings the new convert in, the first individual that one should encounter is the pastor for he/she introduces themselves to that person and hopefully shows their heart to the person as to make them feel welcomed and also show that the pastor is trustworthy. In larger churches this is more difficult because it's a larger number of people but this is where care pastors or Pastor's assistants come in. There are several different names for the people assist the Pastors in the new member process. Often times these are people who definitely have the heart of the Pastor and are knowledgeable of the church vision, mission and foundational beliefs. In larger churches they have groups of people who are assigned to overseers (sometimes they are separated by alphabet, or other methodologies but the process is about the same.

> ➤ The new convert comes in
> ➤ The church secretary or administrator gets their name and contact information
> ➤ They are assigned to their group and leader
> ➤ The leader contacts them in a reasonable amount of time and introduces themselves and sets up a meeting for them to share the vital statistics of the ministry and to get acquainted. If the caregiver is really good then he/she will have regular fellowships with the members of their group to build relationship and rapport and to foster a sense of belonging which would promote more dedication and member activity in the church as well. We all know that in ministries that are the size of churches like Lakewood and the Potters House, it is virtually impossible for the Pastor to reach out to all of those members and often people join these churches for their ministry effectiveness. There is also the chance of these people feeling disconnected and overlooked so this sort of structure would be beneficial for individuals like this. Many churches also have flow charts that look something like this that helps with the church organization

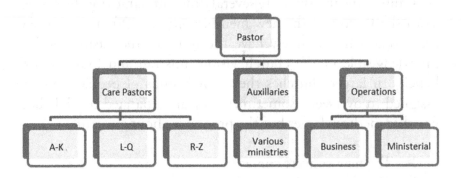

How do they generally operate?

Pastors are generally authoritative people.

Notice that I said authoritative and not authoritarian. This is key because authoritative people honor leadership and authority in a manner that is respectful and courteous with a team player mentality, whereas the authoritarian is one who usurps authority and throws their weight around in expectation that the people will follow them because of their title and not the earning of the respect of the people. The problem is or could be that many Pastors expect respect because of their name wherein they have to understand that this is something that one must earn. I personally am one who sits back and watches the life of a person before I bestow my trust and respect in them. I watch how their family is, do they respect them? Do the other members respect him? What is the word on the street about them? When I tell people what church I go to and who my Pastor is what the response is?

Why are they so vital to the Body of Christ?

Pastors are vital to the body because they are spiritually assigned to us (lay people) as a spiritual shepherd to ensure that the sheep are not being led astray nor are they being eaten by wolves. In my marital counseling that I perform I always say as I was taught that there are 5 p's that the husband is supposed to be to the wife and this is an instance where these same 5 p's can be used.

- ➢ Priest
- ➢ Prophet
- ➢ Pal
- ➢ Provider
- ➢ Protector

The Pastor should be these same things to the flock. Understand the priest was used to submit prayers to God on behalf of the people, the prophet returned the word from the Lord, the provider in him provides instruction on Christian living and should actually echo the words of the other members of the five-fold ministry especially the teacher and the prophet. The Pastor is also responsible for protecting us from false winds and doctrines by ensuring that the people that he allows in the church are authentic and not soothsayers or saying or doing things to lead us astray. Most of all a Pastor should be personable an approachable. We still need to know that they are human and are able to make mistakes. I believe that the more transparent a pastor is the more effective he or she becomes. No one wants to hear from a person who claims to be perfect especially when we can clearly see that their life is far from it.

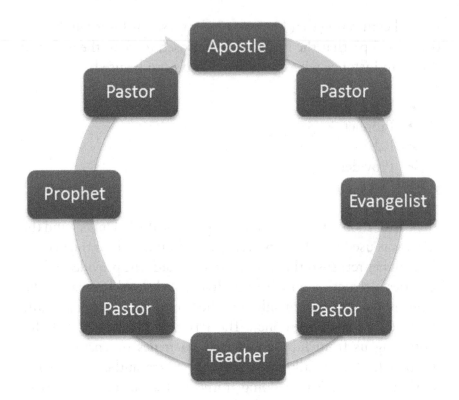

As you can see from the diagram above, the Pastor can easily be overtaken with stress and frustration if he/she does not remain prayed up and in tune with what the spirit of God is saying. The Apostle passes instruction down to the Pastor; the Pastor gives instruction to the evangelist who will report back to the Pastor with new converts who will encounter the Pastor. The Pastor will in turn brief the teacher on what needs to be taught in the spiritual development process. During this interim the Prophet comes into the picture and further directs the Pastor in what the Lord is saying for the body and then the Pastor turns and informs the Apostle of the direction in which the church is going. At the end of the day, the Holy Ghost should be in the midst to bring all things together in line and on one accord. In other words no one should be blindsided by the directions given both by the Apostle or the Pastor and certainly not from the prophet because prophecy only comes to confirm what God has already said to an individual.

Qualifications

1Peter 5:2-4

2Feed the flock of God which is among you, taking the oversight thereof, not by constraint, but willingly; not for filthy lucre, but of a ready mind;

3Neither as being lords over God's heritage, but being ensamples to the flock.

4And when the chief Shepherd shall appear, ye shall receive a crown of glory that fadeth not away.

Jeremiah 3:15

15And I will give you pastors according to mine heart, which shall feed you with knowledge and understanding.

- Team player
- Manages his/her home well
- Has his personal affairs in order
- Has an honorable name in the community
- Able to delegate authority as he/she is given direction from the Lord!

EVANGELIST

EVANGELIST

What is it?

A person who travels from place to place, preaching the Gospel (2 Timothy 4:5)

> *5But watch thou in all things, endure afflictions, do the work of an evangelist, and make full proof of thy ministry*

Where are they located? Significance?

The evangelist is the middle finger because it reaches the furthest distance to bring the people in. Evangelist **ARE NOT** "house people". They are the ones who are assigned by God to go out and compel people to come in. This job is shared by the masses, we are all responsible for doing this but this is their office and their call and they are to teach others how to effectively do it as well.

Personal Attributes-

Personable, very hospitable, wordy (able to talk with vision and purpose for the sake of souls), proficient in the word of God

Who are some in the Bible?

Philip (Acts 21)
Moses (Hebrews 3)
Micaiah (2 Chronicles 18)
Azariah (2 Chronicles 26)
Balaam (Numbers 22-24)
Nathan (2 Samuel 12)
Isaiah (Isaiah 39)

When should a new convert encounter them?

The Evangelist is oftentimes the first person that a new convert encounters seeing as it is primarily the evangelists' job to bring in the flock. They will often time be the one that the new members lean on the most.

How do they generally operate?

The work of the evangelist is never done in that because they are the first person that new members encounter they are often the ones with the longest lived relationship. With that being said they have to make sure that the people are well versed on the role of the evangelist and understand the fact that they are not going to be in sight all the time nor are they always available but are still very much present.

Why are they so vital to the Body of Christ?

Evangelists are vital to the body in the fact that they are the primary individuals to grow the body. If there are no evangelist in the body then who will teach the lay members of the correct way to attain and retain members. The teacher could complete this task but if the teacher is assigned to the education of the household on the various levels of ministry and development and there are no opportunities for application under the supervision of the individual who is experienced in that office how can the instruction be effective.

Qualifications

2 Timothy 4:5 (KJV)

But watch thou in all things, endure afflictions, do the work of an evangelist, make full proof of thy ministry.

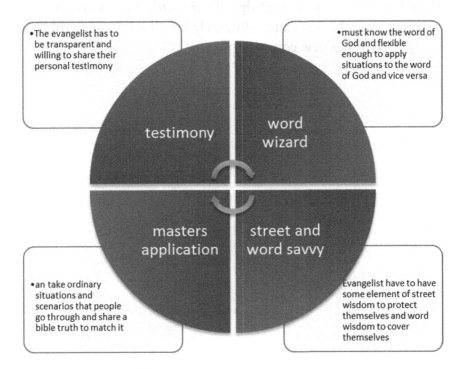

- The evangelist has to be transparent and willing to share their personal testimony

- must know the word of God and flexible enough to apply situations to the word of God and vice versa

testimony

word wizard

masters application

street and word savvy

- an take ordinary situations and scenarios that people go through and share a bible truth to match it

Evangelist have to have some element of street wisdom to protect themselves and word wisdom to cover themselves

Above are just some of the vital attributes that an evangelist needs to be successful in their ministry. The interesting thing is that when they are filled with the Holy Ghost most of these attributes are met simultaneously. In all of the gifts it is vital to have a personal prayer and devotion time but especially in the evangelistic world. I was always taught and I always teach that we should study to live and not to preach because when you study to live preaching becomes easy. I remember one time I was under the tutelage of a man of God and for a season he would tell us, "If you can't cite the scripture, don't say the scripture!" That was a time when I became very proficient in citations as I grew in the faith and continued in the business of my schedule I realized that the best way to facilitate or foster a hunger for personal devotions so now the methodology that I use is that I give them the book that the scripture is enveloped in and have them search for it, this works if time permits but in the middle of in-depth studies I will cite the addresses. For the purposes of the evangelistic ministries, there has to be a true knowledge of the word, there is no time for faking it to make it because ultimately it will kill your credibility in the face of the new converts.

PROPHET

Prophet (ess)

***Prophetess is the name for female prophets**

What is it?

An inspired messenger called by God to declare his will

Ezra 5:2

2Then rose up Zerubbabel the son of Shealtiel, and Jeshua the son of Jozadak, and began to build the house of God which is at Jerusalem: and with them were the prophets of God helping them.

Described as God's Servant

Zecharaiah 1:6

But my words and my statutes, which I commanded my servants the prophets, did they not take hold of your fathers? and they returned and said, Like as the Lord of hosts thought to do unto us, according to our ways, and according to our doings, so hath he dealt with us.

Watchmen
<u>**Ezekiel 3:17**</u>

*Son of man, I have made thee a watchman unto
the house of Israel: therefore hear the word at my
mouth, and give them warning from me.*

<u>*Where are they located? Significance?*</u>

The prophet is the pointer finger because they direct the body
which way they are to go. When God wants to speak authentically
to his people, though he speaks to all of us in his own way, he uses
the prophet primarily to speak to the body corporately, but also
individually.

<u>*Personal Attributes-*</u>

Prophets are not socialites, they would prefer to be alone most of
the time. They are often misunderstood and people don't care to
be around them because people shy away from them due to fear.
On the same token though some people like to be around prophets
because;

- They provoke them to think deeper
- They want to prostitute the foretelling gift of prophesy

Who are some in the Bible?

Males	Females
Isaiah (The book of)	Miriam (Exodus 15:20)
Ezekiel (The book of)	Deborah (Judges 4:4)
Jeremiah (The book of)	Huldah (2 Kings 22:14)
Elijah (1 and 2 Kings)	Anna (Luke 2:36)
Moses (Exodus 3, 4, 6, 7, 17, 19, 33)	Noadiah (Nehemiah 6:14)
Obadiah (The book of)	Elizabeth (Luke 1:41-55)
Nathan II Samuel 7:12-17 12:1-25	Daughters of Philip (Acts 21:9)

When should a new convert encounter them?

A new convert's first experience with the prophetic should be within their local church wherein the five-fold ministry gifts are properly established and functioning where all 5 offices are filled and flowing freely. Such a setting provides the nurturing environment conducive for biblical growth and development as well as establishes the boundary of safety.

Proverbs 11:14

*14Where no counsel is, the people fall: but in
the multitude of counsellors there is safety*

How do they generally operate?

Many people have taught on the prophetic and many have their perspective as to the types of prophets and the manners in which they operate.

This was taken from Chuck Pierce's Notes

6 Types of Prophetic Streams

1. Nabi (Bubble Up)-Unction from within to Vocalize. Flow. Water.
2. Roeh (Seer)-Discernment. Seeing on people, through people. Dreams.
3. Shamar (Watchman)-See Gods Timing, When Things will happen.
4. Chozeh (Vision)-Going into a Trance, Open Vision.
5. Prophetess (To Foretell)-Future Prediction
6. Nataph (To Preach)-Tearing Open Heavens Bringing Revelation. Freedom through Energetic Vocalized Prophecies. Fire. Burning.

The R.I.T.A. Now website says;

Ministry starts with a calling and not a desire, and that calling must be from God. A true prophet is not someone trying to become a prophet, he **IS** one. While the school of prophets can be helpful in developing those that have been anointed by God with the anointing of a prophet one cannot simply take a class to learn to be a prophet. Schools of prophets may be helpful; however, they will be counterproductive if they just bring forth parrots who all prophesy the same things.

The office of the prophet and the "one who prophesies" can be any willing believer through whom the Holy Spirit chooses to operate the simple manifestation of the gift of prophecy.

The fact that one is merely used of God to prophesy does not make that person a prophet by any means. Another major difference is that the simple gift of prophesy by a lay believer (non-Fivefold minister) must be limited to edification, exhortation and comfort while the ministry of a prophet is not so limited, but in addition to these may also include: revelation, foretelling of future events, divine counsel, guidance, direction, correction, admonition, and in some cases rebuke.

Different Kinds of Prophets

There are many different kinds of prophets. All who are also teachers (Ac. 13:1).There are prophets whose primary ministry is within a local body. Some prophets are called to be the local resident apostle over a work, giving it apostolic oversight. Other prophets have a traveling ministry, and some function not only as prophets but also as Missionaries (Acts 13:1-4). Prophets are SEERS; they see things supernaturally in the Spirit that other people don't see. 1 Sam. 9:9 . . . Prophets can hear things that are not intended to be heard by others; if God reveals it to them, they can even hear evil plans conceived in privacy and secrecy. 2 Kgs. 6:8-12 . . . Prophets pronounce judgment Jer. 1:16, 17. Prophets can execute God's judgments. Rev. 11:3-13 . . . Prophets expose sin: Nathan the Prophet exposed the sin of David. 2 Samuel 11:1-12:13

When Israel was in trouble and needed a deliver, God sent a prophet. They (Midian) invaded the land to ravage it. Midian so impoverished the Israelites that they cried out to the Lord for help. When the Israelites cried to the Lord because of Midian, he sent them a prophet (Jud 6:6, 7).

Many of the prophets of the Old Testament found themselves confronting kings, and taking an important role in national affairs. Some also addressed their words to foreign nations. They demonstrate the ministry of the Prophet to the Nations . . . A Prophet to the Nations releases God's hand of power. God cannot act, without first giving a warning through his prophets.

JDM Prophetic Ministries identifies prophets in this manner;

The Preaching Prophet

The preaching prophet or "prophetic preacher" is a prophetically-gifted Christian who communicates the Spirit's immediate message in sermon form. He/she does not make a brief prophetic statement then walk away. Rather, he perceives the situational message and reproduces it in sermon form. It may include teaching and explanation on the fringes, but the discourse is driven by a central Spirit-prompted word. And though the prophetic preacher may not tag his words with "Thus says the Lord", the listeners nonetheless walk away knowing God has just spoken.

Some preach concerning sin, holiness, and judgment in the church. These are undoubtedly some of the most intense and confrontational characters. John the Baptist was like this (Luke 3:2, 3).

On the other hand, there are prophets who preach concerning the church's responsibility in society: caring for the poor, needy, helpless, outcast, prisoner, widow, and unborn. These are some of the most tenderhearted champions. The Old Testament prophets intermittently experienced these types of preaching burdens. Some prophets proclaim God's overall program for groups, structures, and locations. They preach what God is saying and doing on a larger, less personal, scale. This helps leaders tremendously to adjust and rearrange according to God's intention.

The possible subtypes and burdens are endless. Whatever it may be, prophetic preachers distinguish themselves from customary preachers through the remarkable relevance, timeliness, perceptiveness, impact, and authority of their words.

The Declarative Prophet

The declarative prophet is a prophetically-gifted Christian who communicates the Spirit's immediate message in a brief statement or statements. Brevity and conciseness distinguish this type from the prophetic preachers.

Their statements can be a word, phrase, sentence, several paragraphs, or a description and interpretation of a vision or dream (Ac 11:28, 13:1, 2, 21:10, 11, 1Ti 4:14). They can be statements of hindsight/past (1Co 14:24, 25; Luke 1:67-75, 1Ki 20:42), insight/present (1Co 14:24, 25), or foresight/future (Ac 11:28, 1Ti 1:18). For this reason, they often write out and prepare what the Lord is showing them, almost like a TV person preparing a public statement.

Declarers, not Preachers or Speakers

Prophetic declarers are not preachers and sermonizers. They make to-the-point declarations. They report the word in brevity and go about their way. If they are not also called to preach, they are highly uncomfortable when asked to "preach" or "speak" and usually do a mediocre or poor job. That is simply not their gift specialty. It is unfair and wrong to expect a declarative prophet to preach if he/she is not gifted and called to do so. Certainly some are also prophetic preachers, but many are not. From what we know of him, Agabus was this type of prophet (Ac 11:27-30, 21:10, 11). He traveled about delivering brief prophetic statements.

The Intercessory Prophet

The intercessory prophet or "prophetic intercessor" is a prophetically-gifted Christian who communicates the Spirit's immediate message in prayer form. Like prophetic preaching, prophetic intercession is noticeably different than basic intercession. Basic intercession is the general practice of praying for others without any intensified anointing for hyper relevance. It is simply "praying without ceasing" (1Th 5:17) and "devoting ourselves to prayer" (Col 4:2). Prophetic intercessors distinguish themselves from regular intercessors (the gift of faith) through the remarkable relevance, timeliness, perceptiveness, impact, and authority of their prayers. Prophetic intercession is directly Spirit-guided and contains a message for the listeners. It is both a prayer and message at the same time. For this reason, one can perceive the Lord's will in a situation by listening closely when such intercessors pray. In fact, whenever I need confirmation or clarity from the Lord concerning a situation, I have made it a custom to seek prayer with prophetic intercessors. I do not directly ask them for counsel or insight or share too much information, I simply ask them to pray freely--and I tune in. The answer is almost always in their prayers, though they might not even realize it! Prophetic intercessors are spiritual snipers. Their prayer targets are specific, seen through a "Spirit scope". They pray like this consistently as a gifting and calling. Their petitions have incredible results for others.

Hannah had a very prophetic prayer in 1Samuel 2:1-10. Read her prayer; it is obvious some of her words have nothing to do with her situation. She even mentions the kingship before it existed (v10)! Many of the Psalms are prophetic intercessions, flip flopping between the immediate situation and something else unrelated God wants to say or do (Ps 16, 22, 45). Habakkuk's prayer (Hab 3) also contains prophetic elements. The New Testament shows Spirit-guided prayer also. Romans 8:26, 27 tells us the Spirit helps us pray. Ephesians 6:18 tells us to pray in the Spirit on all occasions. Jude 20 tells us to build ourselves up by praying in the Spirit. These commands are given to all Christians, but prophetically-gifted Christians will be exemplary and specialists in this area.

The Musical Prophet

The musical prophet or "prophetic psalmist" or "prophetic poet" is a prophetically-gifted Christian who communicates the Spirit's immediate message in musical or poetic form (1Sam 10:5,6, 1Chr 25:1-7, Isa 5:1-7, Eze 33:30-33, Eph 5:18,19 w/Ac 19:6). Like the preaching and intercessory distinction, prophetic music is noticeably different than regular music. Regular music is the general adoration of God or celebration of spiritual truths without any intensified anointing for hyper relevance. It is the music we give Him simply because it is due Him, whether we feel like it or not, whether it seems relevant or not (1Chr 16:29, Ps 29:2). Prophetic music (including poetry) is slightly different and has a slightly different purpose, which is to bless both God *and* people simultaneously (as in 1Sam 10:5-7). Such music is obviously divinely-initiated. Songs like "Shout to the Lord", "Days of Elijah", "Amazing Grace", and many others are obviously divinely-initiated songs that bless God and listener simultaneously. The unusual magnitude of their influence and message signify divine origin. Musical prophets consistently levitate themselves and their listeners into a state of Spirit-filled worship and communion with God.

Musical Prophecy in Scripture

In the Old Testament, 1Samuel 10:5, 6, 1Chronicles 25:1-7, Isaiah 5:1-7, and Ezekiel 33:30-33 specifically show prophetic music. David was the most prolific musical-poetic prophet, writing numerous Psalms containing prophetic inserts, undercurrents, and endowments. In the New Testament, Ephesians 5:18, 19 mentions it, alluding to the Ephesians' initial prophetic praise experience in Acts 19:6 around eight years earlier. Paul mentions it in Philippians 3:3, referring to "worshiping by the Spirit". As Ephesians 5:18, 19 tells us, any Christian can worship "prophetically" or by the Spirit. However, prophetic musicians have the gift and musical know-how to consistently induce this state. They distinguish themselves from regular musicians through the remarkable relevance, timeliness, perceptiveness, impact, and authority of their songs and poems.

Why are they so vital to the Body of Christ?

Amos 3:7 Surely the Lord God will do nothing but he revealeth his secret unto his servants, the prophets.

Each time a prophet approaches the throne, they go to God with an expectation of a revelation to assist them in their declaration of confirmation. I prefer to use the term "declaration of confirmation" versus "prophecy" because that is exactly what it is. When a prophet speaks, it should be something that God has already dealt with the individual about and /or something that someone else has already told them, be it spiritually or naturally. The words of the prophet should never catch one by surprise. Oftentimes, I am tickled by the looks on other people's faces whenever God allows me to speak a prophetic word in their life. Many would think that I have told the individual something that they have never heard of, but the truth of the matter is that they are shocked that I (a complete stranger)

knows their business so well and can be so specific without even knowing their name or any other identifying information.

Familiarize yourself with this diagram below. Notice that the prophet is significantly different and crossed out. The reason and rationale is the face that the prophet is nearly the secret weapon for the body. The Prophet (the authentic ones) only speaks when released by the Pastor or Apostle. This maintains order in the house as is described in

<u>1 Corinthians 14:40</u>.

40Let all things be done decently and in order.

Warning: the safest way for the correct operation of a prophet is in a group. In 1 Corinthians 14:29-33.

29Let the prophets speak two or three, and let the other judge.

30If any thing be revealed to another that sitteth by, let the first hold his peace.

31For ye may all prophesy one by one, that all may learn, and all may be comforted.

32And the spirits of the prophets are subject to the prophets.

33For God is not the author of confusion, but of peace, as in all churches of the saints.

There are instructions given to the prophet in the group. What I love about the band of prophets that are authentic and in sync is that when one gets stuck or unclear the other is able to pick up where they left off and get the point across. It is amazing to watch but it is also amazing to be a part of as well.

There are times when I wonder how it is that churches operate without a prophetic gift in the house. I can't imagine life without the prophet.

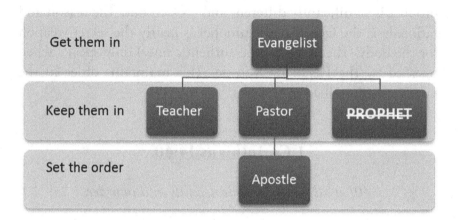

Personality traits of the Prophetic are up to and including

- ✓ Moody
- ✓ Introverted
- ✓ Super hero in the holy ghost but super vulnerable outside of it
- ✓ Emotional in themselves
- ✓ If married, they are often the opposite of their spouse who is completely extroverted
- ✓ Really ok being by themselves most of the time
- ✓ They often have cave experiences wherein they go in one way and come out another
- ✓ Spiritual schizophrenic-walking in the natural and head is in the heavens
- ✓ Often do the opposite of what everyone is doing
- ✓ Indecisive in the natural-they often second guess ourselves in the natural in decision making

✓ Very guarded towards other individuals and rarely let people get close to them

In no way are these the only personality traits there are several more but these are some of the most common traits that the enemy uses to deter and distract you from what really matters, your call and your obedience. I have several prophetic friends and not because I planned it that way but God ordained it that way so that I would not feel bad for not feeding the relationship the way that others need to be fed. *Note, the greatest friend for a prophetic person to have is another prophetic friend because they can hang out today and are not offended with each other if they don't talk again for another month or so. The relationships of a prophet have to be ordained because ordinary people cannot really stand being in the presence of the prophet because they feel as though they have to walk lightly and think right because they feel that you will walk around reading people's thoughts and minds all day and even if you do, it's not intentional and it's not always meant for you to say something to them sometimes it's just meant for you to pray.

Qualifications

- Not trying to win any congeniality awards-you will often times be the most hated so you must be prepared
- Be willing to stand out from the rest
- Be bold
- Be diligent in devotions. People always seek the advice of the prophet for a fresh word because a prophet is one that stays in the face of God at all times.
- Knowledgeable of the word of God
- Insightful
- Wordy but does not talk a lot
- Not rambunctious
- Often times an earthly fighter

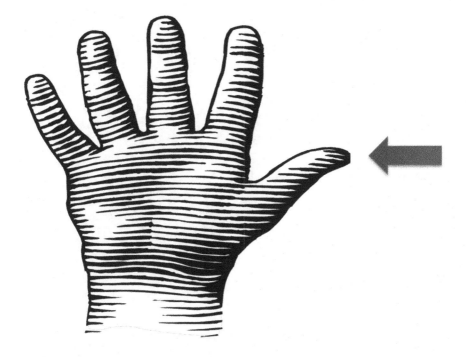

APOSTLE

APOSTLE

What is it?

An apostle is the founder and planter of new churches. The leader and overseer of several ministries (often equated with Missionaries). In Paul's letters, persons who saw the risen Christ and who were especially called by him are regarded as Apostles

Luke 6:13-16

13And when it was day, he called unto him his disciples: and of them he chose twelve, whom also he named apostles;

14Simon, (whom he also named Peter,) and Andrew his brother, James and John, Philip and Bartholomew,

15Matthew and Thomas, James the son of Alphæus, and Simon called Zelotes,

16And Judas the brother of James, and Judas Iscariot, which also was the traitor.

1 Corinthians 15:5-8

5 and that he appeared to Cephas, and then to the Twelve. 6 After that, he appeared to more than five hundred of the brothers and sisters at the same time, most of who are still living, though some have fallen asleep. 7 Then he appeared to James, then to all the apostles, 8 and last of all he appeared to me also, as to one abnormally born.

Where are they located? Significance?

The apostle is the thumb because they are able to operate in all functions but most importantly as the thumb they are able to be utilized as a human touch point and point of reference for matters that may not be understood. Apostles are over several churches and are accountable to each of them. The mantle on their life is great and should not be taken lightly. The Apostle is the heart of the ministry; they are the building block for the ministry as a whole.

Personal Attributes

- Delegates authority and responsibility
- understands and implements order
- follows the rules and makes changes when needed
- personable
- knowledgeable
- accessible
- has a constant ear attuned to God for direction
- manages his own household well

Who are some in the Bible?

The most common apostles were the twelve apostles that ministered with Jesus in the text mentioned above.

<u>When should a new convert encounter them?</u>

The new convert rarely if ever encounters the apostle except on special occasions when he or she comes to the church for some reason but the contact will rarely if ever be constant or consistent. The Apostle is more so for the usage of the leaders but depending on the individual may at times choose to mingle with the laypersons.

<u>How do they generally operate?</u>

Apostles' generally operate in an authoritative manner and are only seen periodically but they still have a silent presence even in the midst of their absence. At any time the Apostle may operate in the other roles of the five-fold but stays true to his primary role as the Apostle.

<u>Why are they so vital to the Body of Christ?</u>

These are they that are the ones who go out and consider a field where there is a need and they build the churches and plant the vineyards.

If we had to rank the giftings, the apostle would definitely be at the heart of the matter. The teacher would be the all-embracing gift whereas they are the ones who train the gifts and operations of them in the correct manner that they are to use them.

Qualifications

The Difference between a Bishop and an Apostle

A bishop is more closely aligned with a Pastor as they are an overseer or elder of a local church in the New Testament times (Titus 1:5-8). The apostle as mentioned before is one who plants churches for others to run under their tutelage.

Apostle	Bishop, Elder, Pastor, Overseer
Internationally known abroad as a clear representation as a covering over a body of believers	Over a local ministry <u>Titus 1:5-8</u> The reason I left you in Crete was that you might put in order what was left unfinished and appoint[a] elders in every town, as I directed you. 6 An elder must be blameless, faithful to his wife, a man whose children believe[b] and are not open to the charge of being wild and disobedient. 7 Since an overseer manages God's household, he must be blameless—not overbearing, not quick-tempered, not given to drunkenness, not violent, not pursuing dishonest gain. 8 Rather, he must be hospitable, one who loves what is good, who is self-controlled, upright, holy and disciplined.

Flowchart for the New Convert

When a new convert enters into the body of Christ, the five-fold ministry gifts become vital to their success. On a norm, the evangelist is the first one that they will encounter. His/her personality and ministry is what draws them in. Then they pass them off (so to speak) to the Pastor. When the Pastor encounters them, it's all about building relationship and rapport with them. He/she then introduces them to the teacher and sometimes the prophet (it depends on the leadership of the church or organization). As mentioned before the prophet is like the secret weapon of the ministry. So they are not revealed until the time is appropriate or until they are released by the head to speak or minister.

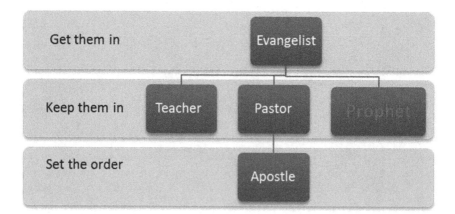

As mentioned before the Pastor is one of the most critical pieces to the puzzle that we call kingdom work. The Apostle normally only talks to the Pastor and gives order for the Pastor to implement. In addition to receiving orders from the Apostle, the Pastor also gets input from all of the other partners in the coalition as well.

Apostolic order is all about protocol and adhering to the proper processes and procedures to get things done. Nothing should be done in the church without the Pastor's approval and blessing because at the end of the day he is the one that is clearly responsible for the body of believers. However, on the same token the Pastor has to be a communicative individual to keep the others in the loop as to what his/her expectation is so that the demands of the people can be met and their personal relationships can be successful for kingdom sake.

Similarities and Differences

This is just a short chart of the similarities and differences between the offices. Again, in no way is this an exhaustive list. Just based on what you read what are some other attributes that you see that are alike and different among them?

	Pastor	Teacher	Prophet	Evangelist	Apostle
Responsible for the body	x	x	x	x	x
Has to be able to teach a comprehensive concept with power and conviction	x	x	x		
Has to be knowledgeable of the word	x	x	x	x	x
Wordy in their calling	x	x		x	
Travels to and fro to operate			X (Sometimes)	x	X
Must be able to adhere to leadership	x	x	x	x	x

COMMON MISCONCEPTIONS OF THE FIVE-FOLD MINISTRY GIFTS

Women cannot be a part of certain offices?

False! As we have seen in this text that there were women in all offices in the Bible. The names may be different (i.e. apostles and missionaries) but they are still very much qualified.

Galatians 3:27-29

New International Version (NIV)

27 for all of you who were baptized into Christ have clothed yourselves with Christ. 28 There is neither Jew nor Gentile, neither slave nor free, nor is there male and female, for you are all one in Christ Jesus. 29 If you belong to Christ, then you are Abraham's seed, and heirs according to the promise.

Bishops, Elders, Pastors, Overseers and Apostles are all the same?

False. There is an elevation and hierarchy for kingdom sake that looks something like this;

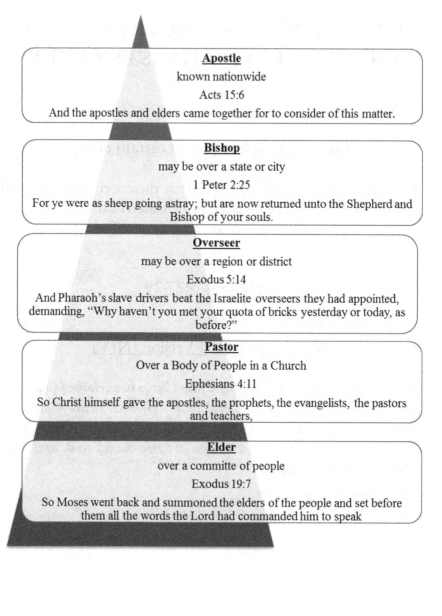

Apostle

known nationwide

Acts 15:6

And the apostles and elders came together for to consider of this matter.

Bishop

may be over a state or city

1 Peter 2:25

For ye were as sheep going astray; but are now returned unto the Shepherd and Bishop of your souls.

Overseer

may be over a region or district

Exodus 5:14

And Pharaoh's slave drivers beat the Israelite overseers they had appointed, demanding, "Why haven't you met your quota of bricks yesterday or today, as before?"

Pastor

Over a Body of People in a Church

Ephesians 4:11

So Christ himself gave the apostles, the prophets, the evangelists, the pastors and teachers,

Elder

over a committe of people

Exodus 19:7

So Moses went back and summoned the elders of the people and set before them all the words the Lord had commanded him to speak

When you are a student of scripture as we all are, you have to pay attention to the details of the text. If these people were the same people then why would he mention them twice in the same sentence? This may seem like a small claim but then one has to ask that how can a sovereign God make such a grammatically incorrect error.

Structures vary according to denomination?

True. There are some churches and/or denominations that have their own doctrine and beliefs. This is where free choice or free will comes in to play. It should be that you attend a church who echoes the same beliefs as you do. There will always be a quarrel of who is right and who is wrong and that is why I was careful to give you scriptures to back up each office and each claim.

NOTE: Whatever you do, do not debate the word of God with anyone, if they walk in error after you have shared the scriptural truth then the blood is no longer on your hands but lies in their personal convictions.

2 Timothy 2:14-26

14 Of these things put them in remembrance, charging them before the Lord that they strive not about words to no profit, but to the subverting of the hearers.

15 Study to shew thyself approved unto God, a workman that needeth not to be ashamed, rightly dividing the word of truth.

16 But shun profane and vain babblings: for they will increase unto more unGodliness.

17 And their word will eat as doth a canker: of whom is Hymenaeus and Philetus;

18 Who concerning the truth have erred, saying that the resurrection is past already; and overthrow the faith of some.

19 Nevertheless the foundation of God standeth sure, having this seal; The Lord knoweth them that are his. And, let everyone that nameth the name of Christ depart from iniquity.

20 But in a great house there are not only vessels of gold and of silver, but also of wood and of earth; and some to honour, and some to dishonour.

21 If a man therefore purge himself from these, he shall be a vessel unto honour, sanctified, and meet for the master's use, and prepared unto every good work.

22 Flee also youthful lusts: but follow righteousness, faith, charity, peace, with them that call on the Lord out of a pure heart.

23 But foolish and unlearned questions avoid, knowing that they do gender strifes.

24 And the servant of the Lord must not strive; but be gentle unto all men, apt to teach, patient,

25 In meekness instructing those that oppose themselves; if God peradventure will give them repentance to the acknowledging of the truth;

26 And that they may recover themselves out of the snare of the devil, which are taken captive by him at his will.

I gave you 2 Timothy 2:14-26 as a reference for the distractions that men will bring to try to deter your destiny to walk in your call. The passages that are bold are the central truths of this passage and should be read with conviction and applied as ammunition to arm you against the wiles of the devil.

THE WARFARE TEAM OF A FIVE-FOLD MINISTRY

To fail to become actively involved in spiritual warfare is saying that we do not care about becomes of ourselves, our loved ones, our community, our nation, and our world! Most Christians have not become engaged in spiritual warfare because they have never been taught the importance of it nor the way to go about it. The five-fold ministry is a vital part to the success of delivering individuals from the attacks of the enemy. When we look at the five-fold the key player is the prophet because they can see and discern what the team is wrestling with. Discernment is critical in all offices but especially in that of the prophet.

- Why is warfare so important
  - o The believer must know his own weaponry and how to employ it and the tactics of the enemy and how to defeat it
- Why would anyone want to be oppressed or possessed and not want deliverance
  - o Embarrassment
  - o Do not want to change

Know this . . .

- A Christian can never be possessed but oppressed! 1 Peter 1:18-19
- No demon can remain when the Christian seriously desires him to go
- You can do warfare spirit to spirit unbeknownst to the person that you are warring FOR!!!

Who are demons?

- Evil personalities
- Spirit beings
- Enemies of God and Man
- Their objectives are to;
  - o Tempt
  - o Oppose
  - o Deceive
  - o Accuse
  - o Condemn
  - o Pressure
  - o Defile
  - o Resist
  - o Control
  - o Steal
  - o Afflict
  - o Kill
  - o Destroy

Structure

- The satanic kingdom is highly organized
  - o There is a prince demon assigned to each local expression of the church

How do they get it in?

- Through open doors
- They have to be given an opportunity
- Sins of omission or commission
- Most enter during childhood
  - The quickest way to understand what doors were opened for demons to enter is to hear an account of a person's childhood

- Through self-fulfilling prophecy

How to know when they are there?

o Discernment-innate sense
o Detection-observing what the spirits are doing to a person

COMMON SYMPTOMS

o Emotional problems
o Mental problems
o Speech problems
o Sex problems
o Addictions
o Physical infirmities
o Religious errors

Seven steps to deliverance

o Honesty
o Humility
o Repentance
o Renunciation
o Forgiveness
o Prayer
o WARFARE!!!

Ephesians 6, 1 Corinthians 13

Basic Understandings That Are Critical To Warfare

o The enemy only has as much power as you give him (Jesus and Satan)
o The enemy can only exercise as much control as you allow him (Jezebel and Ahab)
o Must be clocked at first sight before it finds strength and companionship (iron sharpens iron can go both ways)
o Most warfare takes place in the mind first and then manifest itself
  o (Be ye transformed by the renewing of your mind)

Who are we fighting?

Ephesians 6:12
For we wrestle not against flesh and blood, but against principalities, against powers, against the rulers of the darkness of this world, against spiritual wickedness in high places.

What are we fighting?

o Mindsets
o Strongholds
o Religiosity
o Tradition
o Formality
o Sin
o Carnality

When do we fight?

At all times, the fight never ends!!! As soon as you
let your guard down then the enemy takes over

1 Peter 5:8
Be sober, be vigilant; because your adversary the devil, as a
roaring lion, walketh about, seeking whom he may devour:

• *From before conception in the womb-*

Jeremiah 1:5 (KJV)
Before I formed thee in the belly I knew thee; and before
thou camest forth out of the womb I sanctified thee,
and I ordained thee a prophet unto the nations.

Through child rearing
Ephesians 6:1-4
1Children, obey your parents in the Lord: for this is right.
2Honour thy father and mother; (which is the
first commandment with promise ;)
3That it may be well with thee, and thou
mayest live long on the earth.
4And, ye fathers, provoke not your children to wrath: but
bring them up in the nurture and admonition of the Lord.

Into adulthood
1 Corinthians 13: 11, 12
When I was a child, I spake as a child, I understood
as a child, I thought as a child: but when I
became a man, I put away childish things.
12For now we see through a glass, darkly; but then face to face: now
I know in part; but then shall I know even as also I am known.

Where do we fight?
Wherever the enemy manifests itself

<u>How do we fight?</u>
Ephesians 6:11-24

11Put on the whole armour of God, that ye may be able to stand against the wiles of the devil.

12For we wrestle not against flesh and blood, but against principalities, against powers, against the rulers of the darkness of this world, against spiritual wickedness in high places.

13Wherefore take unto you the whole armour of God, that ye may be able to withstand in the evil day, and having done all, to stand.

14Stand therefore, having your loins girt about with truth, and having on the breastplate of righteousness;

15And your feet shod with the preparation of the gospel of peace;

16Above all, taking the shield of faith, wherewith ye shall be able to quench all the fiery darts of the wicked.

17And take the helmet of salvation, and the sword of the Spirit, which is the word of God:

18Praying always with all prayer and supplication in the Spirit, and watching thereunto with all perseverance and supplication for all saints;

19And for me, that utterance may be given unto me, that I may open my mouth boldly, to make known the mystery of the gospel,

20For which I am an ambassador in bonds: that therein I may speak boldly, as I ought to speak.

21But that ye also may know my affairs, and how I do, Tychicus, a beloved brother and faithful minister in the Lord, shall make known to you all things:

22Whom I have sent unto you for the same purpose, that ye might know our affairs, and that he might comfort your hearts.

23Peace be to the brethren, and love with faith, from God the Father and the Lord Jesus Christ.

24Grace be with all them that love our Lord Jesus Christ in sincerity. Amen.

WHY do we fight?
To inherit the Kingdom of God and to live out our true calling and potential to the glory of God!

Warfare Mannerisms, Elements and Misconceptions

What is the significant of the oil?
For the purpose of protecting the soldier at war praying and the anointing of the recipient . . . olive oil is traditional and biblical but is not a must, water can be used as well as other oils which have been blessed.

Why open the doors and windows?

For sanitary reasons and also to allow a place for the demonic influences to go if improperly ordered in removal

You can catch a demonic spirit?

No, demonic spirits are transferred through various mediums such as sex, spiritual malpractice, and inadequate spiritual preparation.

What is the significance of the towel?

The obvious reasons are for the sweat of the warrior as well as the covering if need be during the warfare process (i.e. a woman with a dress on or if the clothes of the warrior are ripped off during warfare), but another aspect is that when you are doing warfare, you are wide open (as the warrior) and to use someone else's towel that has not been anointed can bring in other spiritual influences that can counteract your efforts.

What is purging?

Purging is the physical manifestation of the spiritual efforts of warfare. It is manifested in ways such as tears, blood and vomit but can also be manifested through violence in which more than one individual will need to partake in the warring activity and immediate backup is needed. It is critical to understand that when an exorcism or warfare is taking place and an injury occurs charges cannot be pressed due to religious rites of passage in the law.

What is purging made of and is it always necessary as proof of completion?

We already covered what purging consists of but under this section I believe that it is critical that you understand the tricks of the enemy concerning this. I have seen the enemy make people throw up their food intake in order for their residency within the individual to stay intact during warfare. Please know that vomit is a manifestation of most emotions, thus being motion sickness and the like but there are times when the stronghold is so deep that vomiting does take place prior to and in the midst of warfare and the spiritual purge can be connected or comingled in with the vomit, this is where the prophet is critical in the warfare process, they should be able to judge the elements as well as the atmosphere and tell you which way to go.

What if people bleed, should you stop?

No. this is another trick of the enemy that takes place, now again this is where a team effort comes in. The prophet is again critical to this process. Caution must be taken but cannot be a deterrent for the deliverance at hand. Remember Jesus shed blood as well for the remission of our sins and sometimes it takes blood to free us again.

When people purge they have to clean it up themselves?

Absolutely Not! This is like making a dog return to their own vomit and eating it. Their bodies are in a weakened state and the residency for the demonic elements are still familiar and will set up residence and of course as we know become seven times stronger than the initial encounter.

All children must be removed from the room during warfare?

Yes or No, this is not mandatory but is a practice. The only significance of this action is for safety, especially if the demon becomes violent and also to prevent nightmares or the like. I for one have never shed my children away from this activity because we encounter warfare so often they would never attend a service.

Who recognizes the demon?

LEADERSHIP!!! Or shall I say AUTHENTIC LEADERSHIP!!! The prophet is almost always the first to recognize it as they judge the atmosphere and then God will direct their eyes to the spirit and the edifice in which it inhabits, then what I like to call the alert roster is implemented wherein the prophet prays that God show the others of the five-fold and hopefully everyone will be obedient and act accordingly. If there are members missing in the five-fold then the prophet should immediately notify the pastor especially if the demon is manifesting itself within the service. Unfortunately there are pastors who won't listen and in that case nothing can be done but just know that you won't be held accountable but the Pastor will.

How can you recognize a demon?

There are so many ways to recognize a demon, the first thing is whether or not you know the individual . . . this will allow you to see firsthand if the individual acts unseemingly. Demons manifest themselves in manners such as;

- Public disruption (talking loud and obnoxiously in service)
- Consistently interrupting the worship experience (this is prevalent is children)
- Many people like to think that you can see the demon in the eyes of the individual or the like and sometimes this is true however, remember that this is a spiritual battle and not a physical one!
- There are also characteristics that are evident in
- Seeking what I call the five-fold of demonic influence
  - o Attention
  - o Power
  - o Control
  - o Jealousy
  - o Strife

Note: you have to remember not to be caught up in emotions nor personal vendettas when doing warfare, you cannot become emotionally involved.

What does it mean to set the atmosphere?
And why is this important?

In order for the activation of the five-fold ministry gifts to operate, the spirit of the Lord must be present because in the presence of the Lord there is liberty and many components are released. In relation to warfare the presence of the Lord SHOULD put the demonic entities under arrest which makes for easier recognition of their influence and presence in the atmosphere. If the entire atmosphere is array then it will be easier for demons to camouflage themselves. In churches where there is no music simply reading the word of God is good enough.

What is warfare in its most basic form in laymen's terms?

The battle between the man and the mantle-everyone has a call of some sort and they partake in sin as a manner of what we call "running" and oftentimes their running catches up with them and has to be dealt with in order for their authentic self to be exposed and the mantle to be apprehended.

Recommended Reads and Resources

(All Scripture references are the King James Version unless otherwise stated)

Churchin' Ain't Easy (Jennifer Gilbert)

Deliver Us From People (Jennifer Gilbert)

Strong's Exhaustive Concordance of the Bible (James Strong LLD. StD)

The Shamar Prophet (Apostle John Eckhart)

The Prophetic Dictionary (Dr. Paula A Price, Ph.D.)

REFERENCES

Bain, K. (2004). *What the best college teachers do.* Cambridge, MA: Harvard University Press.

Brown, K., & Cullen, C. (2006). Maslow's Hierarchy of Needs used to measure motivation for religious behavior. *Mental Health, Religion & Culture, 9*(1), 99-100.

Coley, K. (2012). Active learning techniques in the Christian education classroom and in ministry contexts. *Christian Education Journal, 9*(2), 357-371.

Cox, W. F., Barnum, K., & Hameloth, N. J. (2010, February/March). A nine point lesson plan format for Christian Education. *The Journal of Adventist Education,* 4-9.

Crabtree, V. (2013, April). Religion and Intelligence. *Human Religions.*

Retrieved from http://www.humanreligions.info/intelligence.html

Desimone, L. M. (2011). A Primer on Effective Professional Development.

Phi Delta Kappan, 92(6), 68. Retrieved from EBSCO*host.* doi:10.3102/0034654308330970, http://dx.doi.org/10.3102/0034654308330970

Forte, J. (2009). Teaching human development: current theoretical deficits and a theory-enriched models, metaphors, and maps remedy. *Journal of Human Behavior in the Social Environment, 19*(1), 932-954.

Florida, R. (2012, March). The real boundaries of the Bible Belt. *The Atlantic Cities: Place Matters.* Retrieved from-http:/www.theatlanticcities.com/politics/2012/03/real-boundaries-bible-belt/1617/

Galbraith, D. D., & Fouch, S. E. (2007, September). Principles of Adult Learning. *Professional Safety, 52*(9), 35-40.

Klugman, C., & Stump, B. (2006, May). The effects of ethics training upon individual choice. *Journal of Further and Higher Education, 30*(2), 181-192.

Krejcir, R. J. (2007). Statistics and Reasons for Church Decline. *Francis A. Schaeffer Institute of Church Leadership Development.* Retrieved from http://www.truespirituality.org/

Krejcir, R. J. (2007). Statistics on Pastors. *Francis A. Schaeffer Institute of Church Leadership Development.* Retrieved from http://www.truespirituality.org/

Krejcir, R. J. (2007). Why churches succeed. *Francis A. Schaeffer Institute of Church Leadership Development.* Retrieved from http://www.truespirituality.org/

Krejcir, R. (2007). Statistics on why churches fail. *Francis Schaeffer Institute of Church Leadership Development.*

Lee, F.N. (2001). *The biblical theory of Christian education* (3rd ed.). Cape May, NJ.

MacCullough, M. (2003). Instructional Philosophy. In J. Braley, J. Layman, & R. White (Eds.), *Foundations of Christian school education* (pp.163-181). Colorado Springs, CO: Purposeful Design

Merriam, S. B. (2007*). Learning in adulthood: A comprehensive guide* (3rd ed). San Francisco: Jossey-Bass.

Newport, F. (2012, December 24). In U.S., 77% Identify as Christian. *Gallup.* Retrieved from http://www.gallup.com/poll/159548/identify-christian.aspx

Newport, F. (2013, January 10). In U.S., The Rise in Religious "nones" slows in 2012. *Gallup.* Retrieved from http://www.gallup.com/poll/159785/rise-religious-nones-slows-2012.aspx?refs=more

Olrich, D., Harder, R., Callahan, R., Trevisan, M., & Brown, A. (2010).

Teaching strategies: A guide to effective instruction (9th ed.). Boston MA: Wadsworth

Reese, S. (2010). Bringing Effective Professional Development to Educators.

Techniques: Connecting Education and Careers, 85(6), 38-43. Retrieved from EBSCO*host.*

Russell, S. S. (2006, October). An overview of adult learning processes. *Continuing Education, 26*(5), 349-370.

Schunk, D.H. (2008). *Learning Theories: An educational perspective* (5th ed).

Englewood Cliffs, NJ: Prentice-Hall.

Schoenbach, R., Greenleaf, C., Cziko, C., &Hurwitz, L. (1999) *reading for understanding: A guide to improving reading in the middle and high school classrooms.* San Francisco, CA: Jossey-Bass Schuttloffel, M. (2005). Reflective practice. In S. Tice, N. Jackson, L. Lambert, & P. Englot (Eds.), University teaching: A reference guide for graduate students and faculty (pp.261-268). Syracuse, NY: Syracuse University Press.

U.S. Congregations. (n.d.). Retrieved from http://www.uscongregations.org/what-growing-churches-do.htm

Vasumathi, T. T. (2010). A Design for Professional Development of Teachers—Need for New Policy Framework. *Online Submission,* Retrieved from EBSCO*host.*

Topical Memory System

Christ the Center
2 Corinthians 5:17
17Therefore if any man be in Christ, he is a new creature: old things are passed away; behold all things are become new.

Galatians 2:20
20I am crucified with Christ: nevertheless I live; yet not I, but Christ liveth in me: and the life which I now live in the flesh I live by the faith of the Son of God, who loved me, and gave himself for me.

Obedience to Christ
Romans 12:1
I beseech you therefore, brethren, by the mercies of God, that ye present your bodies a living sacrifice, holy, acceptable unto God, which is your reasonable service.

John 14:21
21He that hath my commandments, and keepeth them, he it is that loveth me: and he that loveth me shall be loved of my Father, and I will love him, and will manifest myself to him.

God's Word
2 Timothy 3:16
16All scripture is given by inspiration of God, and is profitable for doctrine, for reproof, for correction, for instruction in righteousness:

Joshua 1:8
8This book of the law shall not depart out of thy mouth; but thou shalt meditate therein day and night, that thou mayest observe to do according to all that is written therein: for then thou shalt make thy way prosperous, and then thou shalt have good success.

Prayer
John 15:7
7If ye abide in me, and my words abide in you, ye shall ask what ye will, and it shall be done unto you.

Philippians 4:6-7
6Be careful for nothing; but in everything by prayer and supplication with thanksgiving let your requests be made known unto God.

7And the peace of God, which passeth all understanding, shall keep your hearts and minds through Christ Jesus.

Fellowship
Matthew 18:20
20For where two or three are gathered together in my name, there am I in the midst of them.

Hebrews 10:24-25
24And let us consider one another to provoke unto love and to good works:

25Not forsaking the assembling of ourselves together, as the manner of some is; but exhorting one another: and so much the more, as ye see the day approaching.

Witnessing
Matthew 4:19
19And he saith unto them, Follow me, and I will make you fishers of men.

Romans 1:16
16For I am not ashamed of the gospel of Christ: for it is the power of God unto salvation to everyone that believeth; to the Jew first, and also to the Greek.

All Have Sinned
Romans 3:23
23For all have sinned, and come short of the glory of God;

Isaiah 53:6
6All we like sheep have gone astray; we have turned everyone to his own way; and the Lord hath laid on him the iniquity of us all.

Sin's Penalty
Romans 6:23
23For the wages of sin is death; but the gift of God is eternal life through Jesus Christ our Lord.

Hebrews 9:27
27And as it is appointed unto men once to die, but after this the judgment:

Christ Paid the Penalty
Romans 5:8
8But God commendeth his love toward us, in that, while we were yet sinners, Christ died for us.

1 Peter 3:10
10For he that will love life, and see good days, let him refrain his tongue from evil, and his lips that they speak no guile:

Salvation not by Works
Ephesians 2:8-9
8For by grace are ye saved through faith; and that not of yourselves: it is the gift of God:

9Not of works, lest any man should boast.

Titus 3:5
5Not by works of righteousness which we have done, but according to his mercy he saved us, by the washing of regeneration, and renewing of the Holy Ghost;

Must Receive Christ
John 1:12
12But as many as received him, to them gave he power to become the sons of God, even to them that believe on his name:

Revelations 3:20
Behold, I stand at the door, and knock: if any man hear my voice, and open the door, I will come in to him, and will sup with him, and he with me

Assurance of Salvation
1 John 5:13
These things have I written unto you that believe on the name of the Son of God; that ye may know that ye have eternal life, and that ye may believe on the name of the Son of God.

John 5:24
Verily, verily, I say unto you, He that heareth my word, and believeth on him that sent me, hath everlasting life, and shall not come into condemnation; but is passed from death unto life.

His Spirit
1 Corinithians 3:16
Know ye not that ye are the temple of God, and that the Spirit of God dwelleth in you?

1 Corinthians 2:12
Now we have received, not the spirit of the world, but the spirit which is of God; that we might know the things that are freely given to us of God.

His Strength
Isaiah 41:10
Fear thou not; for I am with thee: be not dismayed; for I am thy God: I will strengthen thee; yea, I will help thee; yea, I will uphold thee with the right hand of my righteousness.

Philippians 4:13
I can do all things through Christ which strengtheneth me.

His Faithfulness
Lamentations 3:22-23
22It is of the Lord's mercies that we are not consumed, because his compassions fail not.

23They are new every morning: great is thy faithfulness.

Numbers 23:19
19God is not a man that he should lie; neither the son of man that he should repent: hath he said, and shall he not do it? or hath he spoken, and shall he not make it good?

His Peace
Isaiah 26:3
3Thou wilt keep him in perfect peace, whose mind is stayed on thee: because he trusteth in thee.

1 Peter 5:7
7Casting all your care upon him; for he careth for you.

His Provision
Romans 8:32
32He that spared not his own Son, but delivered him up for us all, how shall he not with him also freely give us all things?

Philippians 4:19
19But my God shall supply all your need according to his riches in glory by Christ Jesus.

His Help in temptation
Hebrews 2:18
18For in that he himself hath suffered being tempted, he is able to succour them that are tempted.

Psalms 119:9-11
9 Wherewithal shall a young man cleanse his way? by taking heed thereto according to thy word.

10With my whole heart have I sought thee: O let me not wander from thy commandments.

11Thy word have I hid in mine heart, that I might not sin against thee.

Put Christ First
Matthew 6:33
33But seek ye first the kingdom of God, and his righteousness; and all these things shall be added unto you.

Luke 9:23
23And he said to them all, If any man will come after me, let him deny himself, and take up his cross daily, and follow me.

Separate from the World
1 John 2:15-16
15Love not the world, neither the things that are in the world. If any man love the world, the love of the Father is not in him.

16For all that is in the world, the lust of the flesh, and the lust of the eyes, and the pride of life, is not of the Father, but is of the world.

Romans 12:2
2And be not conformed to this world: but be ye transformed by the renewing of your mind, that ye may prove what is that good, and acceptable, and perfect, will of God.

Be Steadfast
1 Corinthians 15:58
58Therefore, my beloved brethren, be ye steadfast, unmovable, always abounding in the work of the Lord, forasmuch as ye know that your labour is not in vain in the Lord.

Hebrews 12:3
3For consider him that endured such contradiction of sinners against himself, lest ye be wearied and faint in your minds.

Serve Others
Mark 10:45
45For even the Son of man came not to be ministered unto, but to minister, and to give his life a ransom for many.

2 Corinthians 4:5
5For we preach not ourselves, but Christ Jesus the Lord; and ourselves your servants for Jesus' sake.

Give Generously
Proverbs 3:9-10
9Honour the Lord with thy substance, and with the first fruits of all thine increase:

10So shall thy barns be filled with plenty, and thy presses shall burst out with new wine.

2 Corinthians 9:6-7
6But this I say, He which soweth sparingly shall reap also sparingly; and he which soweth bountifully shall reap also bountifully.

7Every man according as he purposeth in his heart, so let him give; not grudgingly, or of necessity: for God loveth a cheerful giver.

Develop World Vision
Acts 1:8
8But ye shall receive power, after that the Holy Ghost is come upon you: and ye shall be witnesses unto me both in Jerusalem, and in all Judæa, and in Samaria, and unto the uttermost part of the earth.

Matthew 28:19-20
19Go ye therefore, and teach all nations, baptizing them in the name of the Father, and of the Son, and of the Holy Ghost:

20Teaching them to observe all things whatsoever I have commanded you: and, lo, I am with you always, even unto the end of the world. Amen.

Love
John 13:34-35
34A new commandment I give unto you, That ye love one another; as I have loved you, that ye also love one another.

35By this shall all men know that ye are my disciples, if ye have love one to another.

1 John 3:18
18My little children, let us not love in word, neither in tongue; but in deed and in truth.

Humility
Philippians 2:3-4
3Let nothing be done through strife or vainglory; but in lowliness of mind let each esteem other better than themselves.

4Look not every man on his own things, but every man also on the things of others.

1 Peter 5:5-6
5Likewise, ye younger, submit yourselves unto the elder. Yea, all of you be subject one to another, and be clothed with humility: for God resisteth the proud, and giveth grace to the humble.

6Humble yourselves therefore under the mighty hand of God, that he may exalt you in due time:

Purity
Ephesians 5:3
3But fornication, and all uncleanness, or covetousness, let it not be once named among you, as becometh saints;

1 Peter 2:11
11Dearly beloved, I beseech you as strangers and pilgrims, abstain from fleshly lusts, which war against the soul;

Honesty
Leviticus 19:11
11Ye shall not steal, neither deal falsely, neither lie one to another.

Acts 24:16

16And herein do I exercise myself, to have always a conscience void of offence toward God, and toward men.

Faith

Hebrews 11:6

6But without faith it is impossible to please him: for he that cometh to God must believe that he is, and that he is a rewarder of them that diligently seek him.

Romans 4:20-21

20He staggered not at the promise of God through unbelief; but was strong in faith, giving glory to God;

21And being fully persuaded that, what he had promised, he was able also to perform.

Good Works

Galatians 6:9-10

9And let us not be weary in well doing: for in due season we shall reap, if we faint not.

10As we have therefore opportunity, let us do good unto all men, especially unto them who are of the household of faith.

Matthew 5:16

16Let your light so shine before men, that they may see your good works, and glorify your Father which is in heaven.